What God Says About...
LOVE

D S Johnson

J&J Publishing UK

Copyright ©2024 D S Johnson
All rights reserved.

The right of Deborah Sharon Johnson to be identified as author of this work has been asserted by her in accordance with the Copyright, Designs and Patents Act 1988.

No part of this publication may be reproduced or transmitted electronically or mechanically, including photocopying, recording or stored in any information storage and retrieval system without the expressed permission from the author and publisher.

All scripture quotations, unless otherwise indicated, are taken from the New King James Version® © 1982 by Thomas Nelson, Inc. Used by permission. All rights reserved.

J&J Publishing UK
Croydon, United Kingdom
ISBN: 978183809147-7

ACKNOWLEDGMENTS	ix
A Note From the Author	xi
Foreword	xiii
Introduction	1
1 Corinthians 13:4-7	**11**
...And Is Kind	*17*
Love Does Not Parade Itself, It Is Not Puffed Up; Does Not Behave Rudely	*21*
...Does Not Seek Its Own	*27*
...Is Not Easily Provoked; Thinks No Evil...	*32*
...Does Not Rejoice In Iniquity But Rejoices In The Truth.	*36*
...Bears All Things, Believes All Things, Hopes All Things Endures All Things...	*40*
Love Never Fails...	*42*
Loving God	**45**
Loving Yourself	**71**
Loving Others	**97**
Jesus Is Love	**109**
In Conclusion	**119**
The Love Scriptures	**121**

What God Says About Love

DEDICATION

To My Children,

Joash, Cheyanne, Ryan, Isaac, Rebecca, Michael, Nathanael, Daniel, Charis-Ann and Benjamin

The things that are written in this book are written by the Grace of God, from a desire to be a good mother to you all. These things I have learnt, are because God saw fit to place you all in my life to teach me about love; not just about giving it, but about receiving it too. I love you all forever,
Mum.

What God Says About Love

What God Says About Love

LOVE

The word rendered love is Agape in the Greek, which refers to unconditional love through an act of the will.

Love is Patient, Kind, Humble, Trusting, Optimistic, Fearless and NEVER Fails.

ACKNOWLEDGMENTS

I would like to thank my Heavenly Father, My Saviour, Jesus Christ and My Counsellor and Guide, the Holy Spirit, blessing and honour and glory and power be to you forever. Thank you for loving me, for inspiring me, for encouraging me; for giving me divine ideas and motivating me to produce them. I am nothing without you. Thank you for the gift of your love.

My Husband Michael, you really are my knight in shining glory! Thank you for being my husband, my best friend, and my biggest fan. I honour and esteem you; I love you.

To my parents Lorna and Tolmie, I want to thank you for everything you have done for me. Through the hard work and the sacrifices, you have given me everything I need to succeed in life. I appreciate you and honour you as my parents. I love you very much.

My Pastors, Bishop Michael Hutton-Wood and Pastor Bernice Hutton-Wood, I am so fortunate and blessed that God saw fit to place my family into your lives and under your ministry. Your prayers, encouragement and teaching have been invaluable and life-changing, and I thank you from my heart.

What God Says About Love

A NOTE FROM THE AUTHOR

As I typed the pages of this book, and as God taught me through His Word, I realised I was far off the mark. I asked, "What do I know about love?". I realised that I could not love God or people, or myself the way I should. I thought of my family and friends and questioned my actions and words towards them, and I almost began to despair. "I am sorry Lord, but I can't love people the way you say I should." But the Holy Spirit answered me, "No, YOU can't," He said, "because perfect love comes from Me. You do not have the capability to love as I have commanded, because human love is limited by feelings. My perfect love goes beyond feelings and transcends every barrier, all time and all space. You must receive My love first, and love Me. Only then will you be able to love others unconditionally. My love is perfect, and if you have not received it, then you cannot give it."

What God Says About Love

FOREWORD
REVEREND BERNICE HUTTON-WOOD

I have known Deborah for eighteen years. She is first, a follower of Christ, a God-fearing wife, a fearless mother of a blended family of nine, an entrepreneur, and a friend who has become a sister.

She is the author of "Fauna & Friends", a series for children - a fun and yet educational series of books that my grandchildren love & read regularly. I also must confess that it has helped me see animals in a more positive light! She is also an accomplished photographer with a published book on local wildlife, "Birds at Kelsey Park" which is a must for your library.

Deborah has a way of drawing you into whatever she is doing - either through her writing, photography or entrepreneurship. You get the feeling of being part of what is being done. Being a Christian, wife, and mother has meant that over the years, on many occasions, she has had to choose to walk in love; that is, to turn the other cheek, or not to retaliate to situations and people outside of the love of God. I have personally witnessed on many occasions when she has chosen to walk away from situations where she had justifiable reasons to respond in an un-Christlike manner, showing her desire for growth and maturity in Christ. It is this dedication to her faith that has led her to write this book.

In a world where love is based on the disconnected feelings or wayward emotions of the individual, and essentially on the selfish approach to life of "Me, Myself and I", the author shows us, and gives an insight into what love is, and more importantly, 'Who' love is.

This well researched, informative, yet simply written book, defines love, and the importance of loving God first, loving ourselves, and then being able to love others; particularly in that order! It also reveals why we struggle to love in God's way of Agape and gives us scriptural answers to overcome these struggles. Indeed, God's amazing love (John 3:16), is the heart of this book of hope. It reminds us that God's love for us is unconditional and never fails - almost as if God cannot help Himself when it comes to His love for us! He craves a relationship with us, which allows us to love Him, ourselves and others.

Having read this book thoroughly, I can boldly say it is wholesome, and I highly recommend it - a must for your functional library. This book, is a book that will bring and restore hope in a world where love seems to be almost impossible, and as our distinguished author simply puts it,

"God loves you, wants you to love Him, love yourself and love others."

Reverend Bernice Hutton-Wood
MA in Pastoral Counselling, Diploma in Music; Resident Pastor of House of Judah City Church Croydon; Co-author of several acclaimed Relationship books with husband, Bishop Michael Hutton-Wood, including What Husbands Want and What Wives Really Want, 101 Tips for A Great Marriage, 50 Common Mistakes Singles Make, 200 Questions You Must Ask Investigate and Know Before You Say 'I Do' and HWP Bestseller, No Ringy, No Dingy!

What God Says About Love

INTRODUCTION

God is love, and when He created us in His image, He put within us a desire to love and to be loved. God made us this way, so we must look to Him to show us how to love Him, how to love ourselves and how to love each other.

Loving ourselves and other people is not easy, because we are imperfect. We are all born in sin and shaped in iniquity, so we all have the same capacity for good and evil. People make choices, some good and some not. We all make bad choices at times and make mistakes, often with serious consequences, but we must deal with it and love each other anyway. This isn't easy.

Love is the decision we make to do good to people. Loving others requires faith and trust, that the love invested will not be denied or betrayed, because once that trust is broken, healing can take a long time, and the potential consequences can be very painful. Loving ourselves can prove just as hard as loving others. We are often too hard on ourselves, and at times we are our own worst critic.

"Judge not, that you be not judged. For with what judgment you judge, you will be judged; and with the measure you use, it will be measured back to you. And why do you look at the speck in your brother's eye, but do not consider the plank in your own eye? Or how can you say to your brother, 'Let me remove the speck from your eye, and look, a plank is in your own eye? Hypocrite! First remove the plank from your own eye, and then you will see clearly to remove the speck from your brother's eye." Matthew 7:1-5

We can, at times confuse the saying "Judge not…" with criticism. Genuine self-analysis for improvement, (searching your heart to check motives, and self-reflection to align our conduct with the Word of God, by reviewing and judging your own actions), is perfectly healthy. The outcome should be forgiveness, making amends and healing. In fact, the Apostle Paul says,

Examine yourselves as to whether you are in the faith. Test yourselves… 2 Corinthians 13:5

However, continuous self-criticism, meditating on negative words spoken to you or about you, is very unhealthy and dangerous for your mental health. You could become so discouraged that you fail to see the 'good' in anything, and this can lead to more serious conditions such as depression, if left unchecked. It is possible to focus on our imperfections and mistakes, so much so, that we feel undeserving of love. This is usually followed by self-abuse (self-flagellation, negative self-talk). Our words and confessions are powerful. The bible says, "Death and Life are in the power of the tongue." It is possible to talk yourself into a state, where you can't imagine how or why anyone could love you, but it is also possible to talk your way out, using the power of positive confession. It is important to maintain a balanced outlook and attitude, as the extreme either way can impact your ability to enjoy lasting friendships and relationships. The Psalmist said, we are all "fearfully and wonderfully made". This means that God took time, care and attention to sculpt every part of our being, and He said it was good. This simple truth is a good place to start loving God, ourselves and others. It's a lifelong journey to see through God's eyes, and learn how to love, from the One who *is* Love.

The love we give may or may not be reciprocated; people may or may not respond, and that can be painful. So many prefer to hide away and retreat into a personal bubble of protection. But what kind of life is that? How can one truly function in this world full of people without having the greatest connection to them, love? This does not mean you are 'committed' to everyone, no, you can have a basic regard for others, and share a deeper intimacy with a few. Love is highly nuanced and multifarious. In the Greek, the various expressions of love are described as follows:

Agape – Universal Love
Eros – Romantic/Sexual Love
Philia - Friendship Love

Storge - Family love
Philautia - Self-love (not to be confused with selfishness, which 'love' is not).

There is also *Ludus* – playful or flirtatious love and *Pragma*- Logical/Commitment love. I would not describe these as 'Love' per se, but they are essential supplements to the aforementioned. *Ludus* is playful and flirtatious enjoyment, akin to the initial feelings you get after a new encounter, connection or the 'honeymoon period'. By itself, it is not enough to build or sustain a relationship, but it is a necessary component to its longevity. Likewise, 'Pragma', is logical and is not based on feelings, but it is built on values. For example, an arranged marriage based on tradition, or political/royal marriages based on treaties and agreements. It is a mutual decision between all parties to stay committed and is an essential component for sustaining relationships.

People tend to focus on the feelings and emotions that support love as the sum-total of it, but feelings and emotions alone are unreliable as they can, and many times will, change at the first sign of adversity or unreciprocated love. Love can begin with a choice (pragma), and the feelings and emotions follow, and other times the feelings come first, but then a choice is made. Regardless of which comes first, both are needed for 'real' love to establish and thrive.

LOVE DIAGRAM

Later in the book, as we explore God's mind about love, we will see that regardless of the expression, love, in its complete or 'whole' form, has specific identifiers that also define it. The principal focus of this book is Agape. Agape refers to the paternal love of God for man, and of man for God, but is extended to include a brotherly love for all humanity. It encompasses the other loves but is also at the root of any friendship or relationship, and the foundation upon which the love between people, romantic couples and families should be built.

"Though I speak with the tongues of men and of angels, but have not love, I have become as sounding brass or a clanging cymbal. And though I have the gift of prophecy, and understand all mysteries and all knowledge, and though I have all faith, so that I could remove mountains, but have not love, I am nothing. And though I bestow all my goods to feed the poor, and

though I give my body to be burned, but have not love, it profits me nothing." 1 Corinthians 13:1-3

God says, no matter what you do, where you go, who you help, what you achieve, all your talents, all your gifts, who you save, who you bless, all your knowledge and understanding, how well dressed you are, how eloquent you are, how qualified you are; no matter your qualification or titles, if you do not have love for God, love for yourself and love for others, it means nothing. If love did not motivate you, if love did not inspire you, NONE of it means anything. WOW! What a thought! Imagine coming to the end of your life and realising that you had a lifetime, but you missed the most needful thing. The story of Mr Scrooge, (A Christmas Carol), is a good reminder of the dangers of a cold heart. He was a successful businessman and wanted for nothing, but he had neither love in is heart nor compassion for others. Then, in a vision, as he stood on the brink of eternity, he came face to face with the reality of his true nature. He recognises his fault, repents, and opens his heart. The end of the story describes his complete transformation and restoration that also benefitted the entire village. Let us not wait until it's too late, or for something tragic to shock us into obedience. God speaks to us daily about His love, through His Word, through His Ministers and even directly to our hearts. Let us embrace, learn and love, as far and as wide as we can.

'Now if anyone builds on this foundation with gold, silver, precious stones, wood, hay, straw, each one's work will become clear; for the Day will declare it,

because it will be revealed by fire; and the fire will test each one's work, of what sort it is. If anyone's work which he has built endures, he will receive a reward. If anyone's work is burned, he will suffer loss; but he himself will be saved, yet so as through fire."
1 Corinthians 3:12-15

This scripture is very sobering. Everything we do and say matters in this life, and more importantly the 'why' is equally, if not more important; because your why is the evidence of the state of your heart, and only God Himself can see and know it. Therefore, He is the only one who is qualified to judge. He really has all the evidence and the whole truth. My Pastor, Bishop Michael Hutton-Wood always says, "Take the word of God literally!" God's Word is what it is, powerful and sharper than any two-edged sword. It is direct and clear, and anyone can read, understand and apply it in any circumstance. This is a testament to its versatility and diversity. God is clear about love; what it is and is not, and we can take His word at face value on the subject.

In this book, we will explore the scriptures and find out what God says about love. By the time you finish reading it, I hope you will gain more knowledge and understanding of who God is, who we are, and this extraordinary gift.

LOVE

Love suffers long and is kind; love does not envy; love does not parade itself; it is not puffed up; does not behave rudely, does not seek its own, is not easily provoked, thinks no evil; does not rejoice in iniquity, but rejoices in the truth; bears all things, believes all things, hopes all things, endures all things. Love never fails.

What God Says About Love

1 CORINTHIANS 13:4-7

Love Suffers Long...

"From the Greek makrothumia translated 'long temper' and hupomone meaning 'endurance' constancy, perseverance, continuance, bearing up, steadfastness, holding out, and patient endurance."

Isn't it interesting that love's first identifying trait is that it 'suffers long'? I have read the scriptures cover to cover, and I would encourage everyone to do so. There is nothing that gives you a more complete picture of God's eternal love than reading the bible from Genesis to Revelation in order, as you would any book. It may take a while, but it is well worth it. Thankfully, nowadays we have various tools at our disposal to help us access the bible in various versions and languages. I advise you to find a resource that's right for you and get reading! When you do, you will see that since the world began, God has 'suffered long' with mankind and still does. Since the fall, God has been lovingly and carefully orchestrating and working to bring us back to our divine position, as it was before the fall. He does this by giving us His law, by instruction through prophets - men and women of God; performing miraculous signs and wonders by His mighty hand, and then making 'The Way,' sending his only Son to die for humanity. God did, and still does all of this to bring us back to him, and to restore us to right relationship with Him. But what was mankind's response? We sinned against Him and went our own way. The bible says that time and again, "they did what was right in their own eyes," and turned away from God, following their own lusts and false gods. But our loving Father never left or abandoned His children. As you continue to read the text, you will find that every time the people sinned or strayed, God would deliver them. He would rescue them and correct them by instruction, but humans being who they are, fell into sin time and again. Thankfully, at each instance, God's enduring and constant love would restore and deliver them. This is God 'suffering long' with His people!

In other versions of the Bible, the term 'long-suffering' is translated 'Patient' – *able to accept or tolerate delays, problems, or suffering without becoming annoyed or anxious.*

Love starts with patience - <u>waiting in hope, with a good attitude</u>. To truly walk in love, you must exercise patience. It is easy to lose patience when relating and working with others, so we must be mindful and disciplined to maintain an even temper. Temperance is also a fruit of the Spirit. It is a sign that the Holy Spirit is working in and through you and that you are maturing in the things of God. This is a very important characteristic, especially for parents, teachers, leaders, ministers and anyone in authority tasked with training or nurturing others. We grow, develop and learn at different paces. We are all learning and those we lead are also growing. We must be especially careful of reacting badly or negatively in frustration when dealing with the inexperienced or the young. Being patient is difficult and can feel impossible at times. It requires self-control for a period undisclosed to you. You never know in each situation how long you will have to manage or endure, so the ability to be patient is crucial. Learning, and adjusting takes time and the process differs for each person and/or circumstance. It takes as long as it takes to see change, growth, etc. We must strive to be patient in the process. We must fight the urge to lose our tempers, criticize, or become anxious, worried or discouraged. Impatience cannot make time move any faster or transform people any quicker. It can, however, cause hurt and steal joy. It can also break confidence and trust. Think about the last time you were in a situation where someone was impatient

Ingredients of Love
Patience – Love passive (relaxed/laid-back)
In no hurry, bears, hopes and endures all things.
DAKE Reference Bible, 1999

with you? What about the last time you were impatient with yourself? If you spoke to someone else the same way you spoke to yourself, how would that person feel afterwards? Would they be inspired and motivated, or utterly discouraged? When we lose patience with ourselves or other people, it becomes sin. Please understand, it is not impatience that is sin, but what that impatience leads you to do. Impatience reacts, gives up, walks away and abandons. God is very patient with us because He loves us. We make mistakes repeatedly, but God forgives us. He will never abandon us or walk away; He will forgive us and give us another chance to do better. I learned a while ago that when you feel God is far away, it is not He that left you, it is you that has fallen away.

"But each one is tempted when he is drawn away by his own desires and enticed." James 1:14

No matter how many times we are drawn away, He waits patiently on us to obey Him, and to grow into the person he created us to be. We don't deserve it, because God is good and perfect, and we are not, not yet. Our walk of faith is to try daily to live as Jesus taught us, and as the Holy Spirit guides us. This is where 'Grace' comes in. Grace is not the licence to do wrong and keep doing wrong, (it is not a shield for wrong behaviour). Grace empowers us to choose to do the right thing. We do many things daily that fall short, but our heavenly Father is patient with us, and gives us the power and opportunity or 'grace' to change. We must do the same not only with others, but with ourselves.

There are times when we want to change things about ourselves, or our lives that we don't like, but we are unrealistic with our goals. We must be careful that we do not set the bar too high, and then berate ourselves for not reaching it. In frustration we say things about ourselves that God has never said, and would never say, and this makes us feel even worse. Remember that change does not happen overnight; change takes time. Don't be discouraged if things don't happen when you expect, just trust the process. Celebrate the fact that it *will* happen, because you have already made the start.

Impatience is also a lack of trust, where doubt has crept in. Trust takes faith to believe, and patience to wait. People are not perfect, and trust is broken all the time. Our faith is not in people, it is in God. When we believe His Word, and build up our faith through obedience to it, then we can exercise patience with others. Know that God is in control of every situation, so you can be patient and 'suffer long', because it is He who is changing and transforming them, and He who will restore and reward you for your obedience'.

Often, we pray and ask God, or we make our declarations about the things we want to see, but it doesn't happen when we want it to. It is easy at these times, to get discouraged and frustrated and even complain, particularly when your need is great. But you must remember that God's word is true, and if He said it, then He will do it. All good things take time. When we exercise patience with ourselves and in our walk with God, then it will be easy to do the same for others. When we are patient with others, we lay the foundation for building fruitful relationships and friendships.

...And Is Kind

"THE WORD KINDNESS COMES FROM THE GREEK WORD, CHRESTOTES; AND IT MEANS, TO BE COMPASSIONATE, CONSIDERATE, SYMPATHETIC AND HUMANE."

To be kind is to do good and be good to others. Jesus tells us to love others including our enemies, not expecting anything in return, but always showing compassion. Throughout the stories of Jesus' life, it states many times, just before he performed great miracles that he was 'moved with compassion' for the people. Compassion fuels kindness. We must have a level of consideration and concern for the sanctity of human life, so that compassion will move us to act in kindness. I think we can agree that this world could do with a little more kindness.

"By this we know love, because He laid down His life for us. And we also ought to lay down our lives for the brethren. But whoever has this world's goods, and sees his brother in need, and shuts up his heart from him, how does the love of God abide in him?"
1 John 3:16-17

How do you know if God's love abides in you? By your kindness. How can you turn a blind eye to the needs of others after everything He did for you? Jesus tells us to "love one another as I have loved you." He demonstrated His love for us and requires us to do the same for others. The best thing we can do is check our hearts, grow, learn and take every opportunity that arises to be kind. Jesus spoke to us about this in Luke

6:35-36. It reads:

"But love your enemies, do good, and lend, hoping for nothing in return; and your reward will be great, and you will be sons of the Most High, for He is kind to the unthankful and evil. Therefore, be merciful, just as your Father also is merciful."

Kindness is probably the thing most needed in our world but is also the most faked aspect of love. This kind of selfishness is masked with kind words or actions and can be difficult to identify until it's too late. People can say the right things but don't mean it, and their resulting actions show how they *really* feel. Also, some may do nice things but have ulterior motives. It's not always malicious as sometimes people have the best intentions, but they still act selfishly. You will have to discern each case with wisdom, but if you've been on the receiving end of this false kindness, take heart, it is not your fault. You cannot control someone's heart and it is not your responsibility to judge someone's actions. You cannot blame yourself for something that is outside of your control.

Ingredients of Love
Kindness – Love in Action
Never acts rashly or insolently; not inconsistent, puffed up or proud.
DAKE Reference Bible, 1999

"Beloved, do not avenge yourselves, but rather give place to wrath; for it is written, "Vengeance is Mine, I will repay," says the Lord." Romans 12:18-19

Don't insist on getting even; that's not for you to do. "I'll do the Judging," says God. "I'll take care of it." (MSG)

We said earlier that love is a risk, but God himself shoulders it all. He sends us out into the world, commanding us to love others and he says, "Don't worry, my love and grace will sustain you, replenish you and heal you. Don't worry if they reject you and use you, love them anyway and I will look after you and take care of them." Remember, we are His creation; He loves us all, and He chastens and corrects those He loves. The scripture above says don't try to get people back, because they are His people too, and he has a perfect plan for them, to bring them to an expected end, according to Jeremiah 29:11. He also says, don't even get angry with them, or sad or bitter. Not only will He heal you, but He will also take care of them, with exactly what they need. We need to recognise that we belong to God, and everything we are flows from him. If we are connected to the Source, we have restoration 'on tap', and His love and grace will always sustain us.

"And this I pray, that your love may abound still more and more in knowledge and all discernment." Philippians 1:9

We must not be afraid to show compassion and be kind to others, but we must be wise. We must not be naïve to the nature of people, and strengthen our minds and character, so we can function effectively as representatives of Christ, and Ambassadors of The

Kingdom.

"Be kindly affectionate to one another with brotherly love, in honour giving preference to one another…" Romans 12:10

Many of the current philosophies and belief systems today are self-centred, but kindness starts with compassion. This is the ability to recognise and acknowledge someone else's need and be motivated to do something about it. When you show kindness to others, it lets them know that you care, and have taken the time to show it. You also share a little bit of yourself, and that transfer of energy can be 'life' to the recipient. Sometimes, showing kindness requires you to sacrifice something, and it can be uncomfortable. This could be sharing or giving your last or cancelling your plans to be there for someone. Walking in love can be inconvenient, but these are times when you need God's love, and His assurances most. So, stay connected to the Source, and remember, great sacrifice brings great blessing and reward.

> *Ingredients of Love*
> **Generosity – Love in Competition**
> *Not envious or jealous*
> **DAKE Reference Bible, 1999**

Love Does Not Parade Itself, It Is Not Puffed Up; Does Not Behave Rudely

"Humility": the quality or condition of being humble; modest opinion or estimate of one's own importance

Is Not Rude

Love doesn't think more highly of itself than it should, and it is not proud or rude. In the previous section, you read that love is compassionate and kind. Rudeness is the opposite of kindness. It is behaving in an unseemly manner resulting in offence to others. It is also a symptom of a lack of self-control, i.e., saying or doing things out of frustration or hurt, or reacting before listening or thinking first. Rudeness also extends to the inability to recognise and follow social cues and etiquette; not embracing those unwritten rules of conduct in society, or within a particular group or culture. It is a lack of manners and discourteousness and showing disrespect brashly or with sarcasm.

We must all commit ourselves to doing everything we can to overcome it, because love is not rude, nor does it behave unseemly (improper, inappropriate). I heard a statement in a movie once that stayed with me. A man had been locked away from civilization for some years and was now learning to be with people again. Another character, helping with his education, sat him down and told him that good manners is the way we show others that we respect them. I had amazing parents who raised me to have good manners, and that statement resonated with me. Everyone should be respected, whether they "deserve" it or not. It says more about you as a person who is respectful and courteous, and about your quality and character. A respectful person is trusted, invited and welcomed, and our good manners is how we show others they are valued. Your anger or frustration in the moment does not remove or negate a person's value but instead implies that they have little or no value and deserve discourteousness. This can have a negative effect on their self-perception and self-esteem.

Rudeness is an act of the ego, and its actions are 'personal'. Correction out of justice may cause offense but it is not rudeness, much like a judge passing sentence or a manager correcting subordinates. The correction and criticism may be difficult to hear and delivered harshly, but it isn't personal, in fact it is necessary for the good of the organisation or community.

Jesus was never rude or haughty. He always acted from a place of justice, and never acted out of selfishness. He knew who He was, why He was sent to earth, and He spoke the truth. It is possible to speak the truth in love, without being rude. The person may not agree and be offended at your words, but if you were not rude, and your motives were pure, you have done nothing wrong. When you love someone, you will always tell them the truth in love and with kindness, because it is good to be kind.

People with low self-esteem have not yet learned to

love themselves. It is easier to esteem others and admire their gifts and talents, but we find it much harder to love and admire ourselves. We are beings created with a large capacity for love, both to give and to receive. The capacity is God sized and He designed us that way, so he is the only one who can fill it. However, many people haven't connected with Jesus and the love of God, and so, they are ignorant of who they are, and the love God has for them. Until they reconnect to the Source, our source of life and love, they will look for it from others. This can be draining and frustrating for everyone. The thing is, people, however well-meaning and loving, can never fill the God sized hole within. If you have low self-esteem, get into the word of God and find out what he says about you. Discover how much he loves you and the plans in His heart for you. Anchor yourself in His love and allow him to love others through you.

If you are trying to love someone with low self-esteem, know that you are not to blame for their insecurities or how they feel about themselves. Don't take things personally, just love them and let God do the rest.

Ingredients of Love
Humility – Love in hiding
Does not advertise, or parade itself; works and then retires.
DAKE Reference Bible,

Owe no one anything except to love one another, for he who loves another has fulfilled the law.
Romans 13:8

Is Not Puffed Up Nor Parades Itself

Love is *not* boastful, it doesn't 'show off. Pride usually stems from a false, puffed-up or servile image of oneself. It is rooted in the fear that we are not who, or what we think we are, or want to be, so we overcompensate or "puff up" ourselves, hoping to cover our shortcomings. Michael C Johnson said, "it is using yourself as the measuring stick of value instead of God's Word." Being prideful is not just thinking of yourself more highly than you should, it is failing to recognise who God is and who you are in relation to Him and others. It is failing to see yourself as He sees you, and the accompanying behaviour and actions consequently affects everyone, because haughtiness needs spectators. The proud crave attention which they then use as a weapon, - as an opportunity to put others down while promoting themselves. This behaviour causes barriers within friendships and relationships, which adversely affect intimacy. This is because neither party truly knows the other. Having to spend every moment maintaining an ego, gives little time to making real connections and building true relationships. In a loving committed relationship, apologising to your partner cannot be out of the question. Unfortunately for some people, it is, but they would demand it if the situation were reversed. Many relationships and friendships are broken or break down because neither party could bring themselves to say and mean two simple words, 'I'm sorry.' How many relationships in your life could be mended today if you would simply apologise? Or is it beneath you? This is not an accusation, just a challenge to walk in love.

Humility is very hard for some, especially those whose high opinion of themselves has been operating for some time. The opposite of humility is haughtiness or being puffed up and boastful (whether in word or deed). Jesus was never rude, neither did He speak or act from a place of pride. He knew Himself, and because He is God, during his life and ministry he continuously exposed the hearts and intentions of those around Him.

> *Ingredients of Love*
> **Unselfishness –**
> **Love in essence (the core of love)**
> *Never selfish sour or bitter; seeks only the good of others; does not retaliate or seek revenge*
> **DAKE Reference Bible, 1999**

Jesus would use the religious leaders as an example in His teachings. He taught people not to be like the Pharisees, who made an open show of their 'righteousness' and 'piety' but did not know God, and whose hearts were far from Him. He also taught the importance of humility in the kingdom of God.

'*Blessed are the meek (humble), for they shall inherit the earth.'*

Therefore, whoever humbles himself as this little child is the greatest in the kingdom of heaven.
Matthew 18:4

"Surely, He scorns the scornful, but gives grace to the humble." Proverbs 3:34

"For I say, through the grace given to me, to everyone

who is among you, not to think of himself more highly than he ought to think, but to think soberly, as God has dealt to each one a measure of faith."

We should be honest and realistic about who we are, and how we see ourselves, so that we do not become haughty or full of pride. If we don't, pride will lead us to be rude to others and this is not pleasing to God. We must strive each day to temper our attitude as it influences our speech and actions. If we are truly honest with ourselves, we will realise that we are not perfect, and we all need God's grace and His love. As we read the Word and spend time in His presence, we will begin to see ourselves through God's eyes and conduct ourselves accordingly.

...Does Not Seek Its Own

"SELFISH" - ADJECTIVE
1. DEVOTED TO OR CARING ONLY FOR ONESELF; CONCERNED PRIMARILY WITH ONE'S OWN INTERESTS, BENEFITS, WELFARE ETC, REGARDLESS OF OTHERS.
2. CHARACTERISED BY OR MANIFESTING CONCERN FOR ONESELF: SELFISH MOTIVES."

Love does not seek its own. God loves us even though he knows most people will not love Him back and will never accept Him.

"But God demonstrates His own love toward us, in that while we were still sinners, Christ died for us."
Romans 5:8

God loves us, and everything He does is to bring us closer to Him into 'right' relationship, so we can live and 'be' as we were created.

"...always having all sufficiency [adequate provision or supply for any and everything that we need] in all [natural and spiritual] things, [so we] may abound to every good work." 2 Corinthians 9:8 (AMP)

Love is not selfish! There are many people who claim to love others, but they behave so selfishly, that one may begin to question if they do. True love wants the best for others, even if it comes at a personal cost.
It is rational and seeks the best no matter what.

Love takes courage. Everyone is different and people

change. There are very few relationships that last a lifetime. People drift apart, people die, but when you love someone, you love them no matter what. You cannot make them stay or be what you want, and you shouldn't try, that is selfish. When we try to hold on to something, or someone, nine times out of ten, you will end up losing them or it anyway. People are not property, they cannot and do not belong to us, not even spouses or children. If you treat a person like they 'belong' to you, then that is the beginning of abuse. Every human being was created with free will by God and belong to Him only. We are granted stewardship in relationships, and we will give an account to the Father. Your spouse does not belong to you. They are fearfully and wonderfully made by God for His glory and purpose, and of their own free will, they 'chose' to be with you. As a steward, you are to love and care for them, and join with them in accomplishing God's purpose for your lives. Your children are also gifts from God. They have been created to fulfil a specific purpose and they are given to you to be loved, nurtured and cared for. You are a steward and will give an account to the Giver one day. Your job as a steward is to guide and nurture them in

> *Ingredients of Love*
> **Righteousness –
> Love in
> conduct/behaviour**
> *Hates sin, never glad when things go wrong; always gladdened by goodness to others, slow to expose and eager to believe the best; always hopeful and enduring*
> **DAKE Reference Bible, 1999**

Christ's image, not your own. Children do not choose the parents, God does, and He chose you for that child or those children. The best thing you can do as a parent is to give your children back to God. They already belong to Him. Teach and train them in the things of God and the kingdom. A wonderful example is the story of Hannah in the book of Samuel.

"And he had two wives: the name of one was Hannah, and the name of the other Peninnah. Peninnah had children, but Hannah had no children. This man went up from his city yearly to worship and sacrifice to the Lord of hosts in Shiloh. Also, the two sons of Eli, Hophni and Phinehas, the priests of the Lord, were there. And whenever the time came for Elkanah to make an offering, he would give portions to Peninnah his wife and to all her sons and daughters. But to Hannah he would give a double portion, for he loved Hannah, although the Lord had closed her womb. And her rival also provoked her severely, to make her miserable, because the Lord had closed her womb. So it was, year by year, when she went up to the house of the Lord, that she provoked her; therefore, she wept and did not eat.

Then Elkanah her husband said to her, "Hannah, why do you weep? Why do you not eat? And why is your heart grieved? Am I not better to you than ten sons?" So, Hannah arose after they had finished eating and drinking in Shiloh. Now Eli the priest was sitting on the seat by the doorpost of the tabernacle of the Lord. And she was in bitterness of soul and prayed to the Lord and wept in anguish. Then she made a vow and said, "O Lord of hosts, if You will indeed look on the affliction of Your maidservant and remember me, and not forget Your maidservant, but will give Your maidservant a male child, then I will give him to the Lord all the days of his life, and no razor shall come upon his head." 1 Samuel 1:2-11

…So, it came to pass in the process of time that Hannah conceived and bore a son, and called his name Samuel, saying, "Because I have asked for him from the Lord. 1 Samuel 1:20

…For this child I prayed, and the Lord has granted me my petition which I asked of Him. Therefore, I also have lent him to the Lord; as long as he lives, he shall be lent to the Lord." So, they worshipped the Lord there." 1 Samuel 1:27-28

Hannah wanted a child desperately. She wanted to be a mother and I'm sure, also wanted to escape the ridicule of barrenness. But once the child came, she recognised there was a greater purpose for him. She did not keep him to herself, she loved him enough to allow Him to fulfil his purpose. In one of Bishop Hutton-Wood's teachings, he says, that this was "another unusual instance in the Bible, where God worked in partnership with a person. God wanted a prophet, Hannah wanted a son," and they both kept their side of the deal. How many parents could overcome the desire to keep their long-awaited child to themselves, especially after all the hoping and praying. But love is not selfish. It is not about what you want or how you feel, it is about what is best. In the Garden of Gethsemane Jesus uttered in prayer, "not my will but thy will be done." Jesus admitted he would rather not have to go through the suffering and pain of His God ordained task, but for love of God, he obeyed. God's will and the salvation of mankind was greater.

Love is allowing a person to be who they are; loving, appreciating and accepting them at every stage and in any state, while believing the best and trusting God to work in their lives. There are very few things in life that can be controlled; life is full of compromise. We compromise when everyone or no one gets what they want. The best compromise is when both parties agree on what is best for everyone, even when it's not what they want. This is love putting aside our will to ensure the best outcome for everyone.

...Is Not Easily Provoked; Thinks No Evil...

"SO THEN, MY BELOVED BRETHREN, LET EVERY MAN BE SWIFT TO HEAR, SLOW TO SPEAK, SLOW TO WRATH; FOR THE WRATH OF MAN DOES NOT PRODUCE THE RIGHTEOUSNESS (OR LOVE) OF GOD. JAMES 1:19."

Love is not easily angered. It is even-tempered and will never think evil of, or towards the object of its love. Love constantly seeks to express itself and does not wish harm or hurt, regardless of rejection and disappointment. Love cannot think evil; it would never want to cause harm or destroy. It does not seek to harm, because it is kind and only wants what is good. Being easily provoked brings a level of instability to any relationship that can poison it over time. If you've ever been in a relationship or had a friendship where you had to walk on eggshells around the other person, you will know how disconcerting it can be. It is hard to build a relationship or friendship when you can't be yourself completely. That restrictive atmosphere, over time, will become toxic to the soul.

If you are easily provoked, you have a short temper, and it is a matter of self-control. We learned at the beginning of the chapter that Love 'suffers long'. Love is patient; it is not easily rattled or moved by any happenstance or report it hears. It is rational and wise and gives the benefit of the doubt. It will not jump to conclusions but will seek the truth before making any determinations. Even then, it will determine to restore what is lost, and repair what is broken. It never gives up and never fails. Love is not easily provoked, because it sees and believes the best in a person, and makes its decisions based on that. It does not mean that love is blind. There is a Jamaican saying, "Love is blind and nuh have nuh smell!" (Love is blind and can't smell). This love is superficial, and more of an infatuation, where no matter the imperfection, they never see it and no matter the odour, they never smell it. On the contrary, real love sees the true state of a person, and chooses to love anyway.

> *Ingredients of Love*
> **Courtesy – Love in Society (everyday life)**
> *Does not behave unseemly, always polite; is comfortable with and can relate to all classes; never rude or discourteous*
> **Dake Reference Bible, 1999**

This does not mean that wrong behaviour is left unaddressed, no, we must at times correct each other in love. When you correct someone, your intention must be to restore the person and not to punish or inflict pain. Facing a disagreement head on can be difficult and heated, but it may be the only way to resolve it. It does no good to ignore an issue or avoid confrontation altogether; seeking resolution requires a level of confrontation but apply wisdom so it doesn't get out of hand. Correcting each other, is simply another way to express our love for one another. Allowing a person to continue down a destructive path is not love. If, however, a person chooses not to accept your advice or correction, they then must make their own decisions and learn from their mistakes. Remember that love forgives offence and hurt. It does not sweep it under the carpet or say let's forget about it. Love acknowledges the hurt but refuses to let it damage them or the relationship. Love is confident to say, 'You hurt me', but is also confident to say, 'I'm Sorry.'

"...bless those who curse you, do good to those who hate you, and pray for those who spitefully use you and persecute you... Matthew 5:44

For if you love those who love you, what reward have you? Do not even the tax collectors do the same?" Matthew 5:46

Love is refusing to let the worst of a person stop you from loving them. It is giving them the benefit of the doubt until you have a reason not to. Insecure people easily misunderstand or dwell on past mistakes and allow it to create a rift in the relationship. But the bible says:

"Finally, brethren, whatsoever things are true, whatsoever things are honest, whatsoever things are just, whatsoever things are pure, whatsoever things are lovely, whatsoever things are of good report; if there be any virtue, and if there be any praise, think on these things." Philippians 4:8

Don't focus on the past or the negative but focus on the good and the positive. Don't meditate on what could, or didn't happen, just be grateful. Once you can begin to do this, it is a definite outward sign that the love of God is being made perfect in you.

…Does Not Rejoice In Iniquity But Rejoices In The Truth.

Love does not support nor does it enjoy sin. It does not seek to do, nor stays in sin. Love cannot and will not deceive itself or others.

Love will endeavour to be pure and remain pure. It will not rejoice in or glorify sin or iniquity, but will rejoice in truth, purity and honesty.

"To the pure all things are pure, but to those who are defiled and unbelieving, nothing is pure; but even their mind and conscience are defiled." Titus 1:15

We are called to be pure - God's best or His divine purpose or intention for us. The difficulty is that many things appear good but are not pure.

"…because it is written, "Be holy, for I am holy."
1 Peter 1:16

To be pure is to be free from corruption or contamination. The blood of Jesus purifies us so we can be holy before God and live with purity of heart. When you accept Jesus Christ as your Lord and Saviour, you have a new heart and the Holy spirit lives in you. Your behaviour is no longer determined by sin but comes from a desire to know and love Him.

"For you were once darkness, but now you are light in the Lord. Walk as children of light." Ephesians 5:8

Whatever our thoughts or actions, we must do all with good conscience. Many people have corrupt consciences and are unable to discern or value what is pure. Social media is littered with millions of people all over the world offering advice, wisdom and philosophies, and we have the arduous task of sifting through all that sand, to find the gold nuggets that will benefit us. A lot of these philosophies come from a place of hurt and brokenness, so if you take something without verifying the source, you could end up taking on the pain and bitterness, along with the advice.

"There is nothing that enters a man from outside which can defile him; but the things which come out of him, those are the things that defile a man." Mark 7:15

Social media is like a window that is always open, and with the many algorithms designed to bombard you with targeted content, we must be vigilant and protect our minds and hearts. It's not just seeing or hearing the content, it is allowing the content to get into your heart; it is hearing it, accepting it, and applying it to your life that will contaminate and corrupt. Everything we are exposed to, must be examined against the Word of God, to make sure it lines up before embracing it. Worldly wisdom can be pleasing to the ear, and may even yield positive results, but it will only last for a time, or it could yield unexpected

> *Ingredients of Love*
> **Good temper –**
> **Love in character/ personality**
> *Never irritated or resentful*
> **DAKE Reference Bible, 1999**

consequences in the long run.

This Love

The Message translation says,
Love doesn't fly off the handle, doesn't keep score of the sins of others, doesn't revel when others grovel, takes pleasure in the flowering of truth."

- Love does not keep a record of past mistakes and hurt. It does not seek to hurt, get even, or to 'have one over' on someone.
- Love does not seek to intimidate or control.
- Love forgives before any wrong has even been committed and continues to forgive.

"Then Peter came to Him and said, "Lord, how often shall my brother sin against me, and I forgive him? Up to seven times?" Jesus said to him, "I do not say to you, up to seven times, but up to seventy times seven." Matthew 18:21-22

Love does not hold things against others, it operates by the law of forgiveness always.

Who is a God like you? Pardoning iniquity and passing over the transgression of the remnant of His heritage? He does not retain His anger forever, because He delights in mercy. He will again have compassion on us and will subdue our iniquities. You will cast all our sins into the depths of the sea. Micah 7:18-19

God forgives us completely. He removes our sin from

us and according to the scripture, casts it into the depths of the sea. God does not recall our sin and constantly remind us of what we did, and how much he has forgiven us. God says, "Forgive as I have forgiven you, do not keep a record of the wrongs, and I will repay." He tells us to put the weight on him. The weight of our expectations, our rejections, our unresolved ego, our disappointment, our dissatisfaction, the behaviours and offences of others, etc.

"Love as I've told you and I will take care of you and everything else."

...Bears All Things, Believes All Things, Hopes All Things Endures All Things...

Love is a choice not just feelings. The feelings you have, come and go; their survival depends upon circumstances (at times when circumstances change, so do feelings). Choice is what remains when feelings wane or are gone, the choice and commitment to love, unaffected by circumstances feelings or behaviour. A couple happily married for thirty years have not stayed together because of how they 'feel' about each other. They stayed together because they chose to love each other through everything; through anger, hurt, misunderstandings, they chose to love and not to leave; to be patient and kind with each other. They did not give up, but they chose to persevere and keep the commitment they made to each other.

Love will never give up hope that it will be fully satisfied, no matter the person or circumstances – New Living Translation

Love bears up under anything and everything that comes, is ever ready to believe the best of every person, its hopes are steadfast and fadeless under all circumstances, and it endures everything [without

weakening]. - *Amplified Bible*

Love: Trusts God always, always looks for the best, never looks back - *Message Bible*

These are paraphrases of alternate versions of the same scripture. It is a good study habit to examine and compare a verse in different translations. This can give deeper insight and clarity to the text.

Love is robust. It can bear all things, it always believes, never gives up hope and is powerful enough to endure. It has the capacity to handle anything thrown at it, and that is where its power lies. All things become possible, because the faith that love activates, is pleasing to God, and this fuels great miracles and wonders in our lives. A mother's love for her children and a desire for their safety, success and welfare, activates her faith to pray for them. This pleases God, and angels are continuously dispatched to watch over and aid them. The same is true for a praying husband or wife. This desire will not fade, in fact it will intensify the more you connect with God. Remember God loves them even more than you do, and he will use you to pray His will for them, not just your fears and desires. Prayer is a vital asset for endurance. Constant communication with God will strengthen and sustain you, not to mention replenish and restore you, as you endure and bear up against the various tribulations the enemy will muster against you. Total reliance on God's love will empower us to last where we would otherwise falter or fail.

Love Never Fails...

Love never gives up, never loses faith, is always hopeful, and endures through every circumstance. When everything else crumples under the pressures of life, or pressure from people, rest assured, love will not. Many are fearful because they have been let down by people that have claimed to love them. This could be a parent, relative or a friend. Agape love, God's love, will never waver or weaken. As His children, it is our eternal goal to love in this way. Only by doing so will fear cease to rule our lives. To love fearlessly, and know that someone fearlessly loves you, will give the greatest peace and security, and fear has no place or power.

Just imagine knowing that no matter how bad things get, the wrongs you've done, whether you get sick, get rich or lose all your money or accomplishments, Love will bear you up, believe in you, never give up hope and never abandon you.

Ingredients of Love
Sincerity – Love in profession (chosen life work/service)
Never boastful or conceited; not a hypocrite; always honest, not leaving the wrong

It's amazing to learn that someone loves you just like that. God certainly does, even more than this book could ever describe. God's love is awesome, amazing and at times, unbelievable, which is why you can only receive it by faith. Faith is being sure of the thing that you hope for, and that 'surety' is your evidence that you have the thing you hope for. Do you know that God loves you so fiercely, that nothing you do or say can change it?

For I am persuaded that neither death nor life, nor angels nor principalities nor powers, nor things present nor things to come, nor height nor depth, nor any other created thing, shall be able to separate us from the love of God which is in Christ Jesus our Lord. Romans 8:38-39

Did you know that when you ask Him, He will forgive all the mistakes and failures, and restore you completely? Then be sure of it! Feelings are irrelevant, believe it!

Love is everlasting. When it is all said and done, love is what it is, and it never fails. Love is always seeking, always believing and always enduring; always humble always kind, always selfless. Did you notice the word always? The word 'Always' is - past, present and future all in one. Which is why we say 'Love is', not was, or will be. Love 'is', and when you choose to love it becomes always. To try and illustrate this point further, consider this, do you love someone you can't imagine not loving? Does it feel as if you have always loved them? Can you imagine 'not' loving that person? Love, by its nature, is eternal. It operates outside time and space and remains even after a person is gone from this life. It is a mystery of God which could be explored further. But for now, know that God **always loves** you, and nothing can separate you from that love.

What God Says About Love

LOVING GOD

With All your Heart, Soul and Might

We don't have to try to figure out how to love God by ourselves. God has expressed His love for us in various ways, and He declares His love in His Word. The Bible is also God's instruction on how He wants to be loved and how we must love others. It is the blueprint of how we must construct lives that are pleasing to Him and fulfilling for ourselves.

When we examine these instructions, it may seem overwhelming and even impossible, but God sent Jesus Christ to be our example, and He gave us the Holy Spirit to be our teacher and guide. A child shows a parent love in various ways, but one way desired above all is their trust and obedience. When a child listens and does as the parent says, it is an act of love; they obey and trust because they are loved.

Gary Chapman taught us about the 5 Love Languages in his acclaimed book of the same name. He breaks down expressions of love as love languages:

Acts of Service - To serve is to surrender yourself or your time to attend to the needs of others.

Words Of Affirmation – Encouraging, positive, kind, honest, and praising words are life to the hearer.
Quality Time – Giving your full, undivided attention.
Physical Touch - Physical presence and accessibility. It provides a sense of security and belonging which satisfies our emotional need to be accepted.
Giving/Receiving Gifts – Visual, tangible expressions of Love

Speaking God's Language

- *Acts of Service*

Serving in the Kingdom – in your family, local church, marketplace, community or internationally in a missionary capacity

- *Words of Affirmation*

Confessions and declarations of worship in line with the Word of God

- *Quality Time*

Devotion to prayer, the reading and study of the Word and spiritual meditation in line with the scriptures

- *Physical Touch*

Seeking the manifest presence of God through worship and sharing God's love with others through kindness

- *Giving/Receiving*

Tithing, giving regularly, sowing financial seeds, and donating time and material possessions.

To enjoy friendships and relationships we must learn each other's love language. Most people do this without thinking about it. The more time you spend with someone, the more you learn about what pleases them and what doesn't. I know my friend enjoys prawns, so when I'm planning a surprise for her, I'll look for the best seafood restaurants and not what I prefer.

God's love language is detailed in His Word. I encourage you again to read this detailed love letter written just for you, so you will learn just how great He is, and of His everlasting love for you. God's love is both universal and unique. The expressions of love between God and myself may differ for you and Him. It is so vast and unending, it is incomprehensible to imagine that God has a tailor-made relationship with every person who ever lived, but he does! It is a wonder of an amazing God, and a mystery we may never fully understand. He belongs to everyone wholly, individually and simultaneously. He maintains innumerable relationships, giving each one his full and undivided attention, and complete love and affection. The sacrifice of Jesus and the power of the Holy Spirit both ignites and sustains it.

In Deuteronomy 6:5, God says:
"You shall love the LORD your God with all your heart, with all your soul, and with all your strength."

He says, first things first, "Love me." Love me with everything you are, as I have loved you with everything I Am. The first commandment says, "Do not have any other Gods before Me." To love God is to place Him first in everything. If you have been in a relationship, you know how important it is to be a priority in your partners life. This desire grows the longer you are together and is cemented in marriage. You are each other's priority. Where there are children, they are the priority for you both, but God is priority over all. The truth is, everything we are and have, was given to us by God our Creator and Father, so they cannot be placed above him. The gift is not greater than the giver. In Exodus 34:14, God tells us he is 'jealous', and will not be satisfied with just a 'part' of us. Would you be content to share your partner's heart with another; endlessly competing for affections, and having to be satisfied with part-time affection? Unfortunately, many treat God this way. We show up when we are hurt or in trouble, and God in His grace and mercy will deliver us, but as soon as the storm passes, we return living as if he doesn't exist. How long do you think the relationship would last, or what would be the quality of the relationship if we treated our partner or spouse like that.

"For God so loved the world that He gave His only begotten Son, that whoever believes in Him should not perish but have everlasting life." John 3:16

God loved us so much, that he gave up the most precious thing to Him as a sacrifice, that through the death of His beloved Son, everyone else would finally and eternally be free, to have the deep and personal relationship with Him he created us to have.

"Now hope does not disappoint, because the love of God has been poured out in our hearts by the Holy Spirit who was given to us. Romans 5:5

...but God demonstrates His own love toward us, in that while we were still sinners, Christ died for us." - Romans 5:8

He desires for us to live in Him and stay in His love. Jesus says,

"...that when you do, I will love you and manifest myself to you." John 14:21

Let's make that conscious decision to love God and express it daily, not in a mechanical, functional way, but as He desires, with all our love, might and strength.

"If you love Me, keep My commandments." John 14:15

"He who has My commandments and keeps them, it is he who loves Me. And he who loves Me will be loved by My Father, and I will love him and manifest Myself to him." John 14:21

"As the Father loved Me, I also have loved you; abide in My love. If you keep My commandments, you will abide in My love, just as I have kept My Father's commandments and abide in His love". John 15:9-10

So how can we love God? What is the love trifecta?

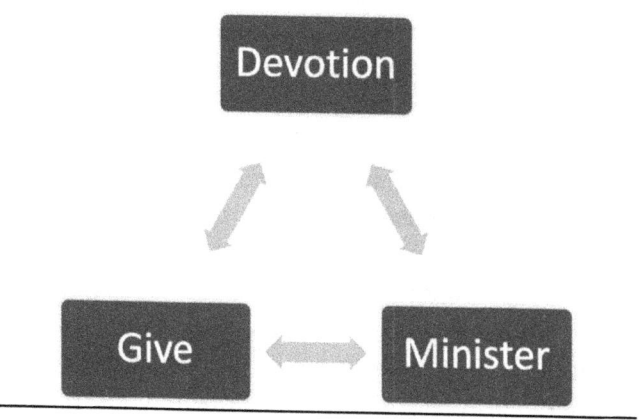

Devotion

How we live our lives daily, is an offering of worship to God. How we think, feel and behave either glorifies God, or is sin against him. We are not perfect, and we won't always get it right, but 1 John 1:9 says,

"If we confess our sins, He is faithful and just to forgive our sins and to cleanse us from all unrighteousness."

Communication is essential for every relationship. Devotion is the time you spend in communion with God. It can take the form of prayer, reading the scriptures, praise, meditation, etc. Regular communication with God, through Jesus Christ is essential for developing intimacy with Him, as well as building your faith. We must have and maintain constant communication with our heavenly Father. *"Pray without ceasing." – 1 Thessalonians 5:17*

Any who come to God must believe that HE is, and that He is a rewarder to those who diligently seek Him. We must not fear or be uneasy to come before God. He is our loving Father, and He invites us into his presence. It takes faith to pray, and when we believe that God is, and Jesus is who He said He is, then we can boldly make our requests, and commune with Him. This must be your mindset of you are to have a successful prayer life. If every time you go to pray, you doubt that God is real, or whether He will hear you, or you doubt yourself with questions like, "Am I praying properly?" Or "it doesn't sound like that sister or that brother's prayer," you will sabotage your prayers before you've even started! We must be rest assured that God loves us, and He is always interested in what we have to say. The more we talk with Him, the more we will get to know him, and our communication with Him will develop over time. The journey of a child's conversation is varied and interesting if you look closely. It starts with crying, then gurgles, and then sounds and laughter, then single words, then short sentences, and then longer sentences, and on and on, until they can have a conversation. Initially, it is about them communicating with you, but as they grow and they develop, it becomes more about meaningful conversations. Prayer is a journey. The key is to be consistent. Another wonderful thing to take note of is that throughout the journey, the parent is always interested in what the child has to say. They are attentive, fascinated and marvel at every new stage in their child's development. Every new sound or word brings joy, and this gives the child confidence to keep talking. God reassures us often in His word about prayer and He encourages us to come to him always.

Read Your Bible... But why?
God is His Word, and His Word is Him. God has said everything he is going to say, and anything He says to us directly, whether audibly or to our hearts will correspond with what has already been written. So why must we read the Bible?

1. To learn the 'fear' of the Lord. God is Holy and must be revered.
...that they may learn to fear Me... Deuteronomy 4:10

2. To build your faith
So, then faith comes by hearing, and hearing by the word of God. Romans 10:17

3. To teach our children and pass on the knowledge of God and the faith. Reverence for God can be taught.
...that they may learn to fear Me all the days they live on the earth and that they may teach their children. Deuteronomy 4:10

4. To be effective in our calling and purpose. We are called and ordained by God for His purpose, so we must have the word of God planted in our hearts and minds, so we do not misrepresent Him.
I will raise up for them a Prophet like you from among their brethren, and will put My words in His mouth, and He shall speak to them all that I command Him. And it shall be that whoever will not hear My words, which He speaks in My name, I will require it of him. But the prophet who presumes to speak a word in My name,

which I have not commanded him to speak, or who speaks in the name of other gods, that prophet shall die.

5. To help you to Pray effectively. To be successful in prayer, we must pray according to God's Word. We cannot do this if we don't know His Word. Jesus taught us to pray that God's Kingdom 'come', and God's will be done on earth as it is in heaven. God's written word *is* His will; His will for us, the church and the world.

Give

There are three main ways in which we give. We give our time, our talents and our resources. Showing our love by giving, is a key identifier or an outward expression of love's attribute, kindness. Three out of the 5 love languages fall directly into one of those categories.

TIME	TALENT	RESOURCES
Quality Time	Acts of Service	Giving Gifts

To show love, giving must be part of our makeup. John 3:16 says,

"For God so loved that he gave His only Son."

Why? So that we won't perish; so that we will have the opportunity to live in full communion with him, eternally in his presence. As stated previously, we are created of love to be loved, and to love, but we became alienated from God and fell from our rightful place. But God's love for us is so powerful and so deep, that ever since then, he has been fighting for us; always working and orchestrating the universe to bring us back to our original state of purity and light in Him. He does this all so that he can commune with us wholly and completely, and to have a relationship with us.

Giving demonstrates our kindness (Agape), and consistent giving shows our commitment (Pragma). God knows our heart, but people cannot see our heart. They can only know us by our actions and what we produce. Matthew 7:16 says:

You will know them by their fruits. Do men gather grapes from thornbushes or figs from thistles?

To further illustrate the power of commitment, consider the following. A gesture every now and again, grand or not, is nice and welcomed at times. Spontaneity is a good boost for all relationships and friendships. But consistency is the real proof of love. The reason we are encouraged to work at our relationships, businesses and education is because there is no substitute for consistency. You must be present and active on a regular basis, giving your best effort to achieve your desired outcome. The proof you are committed at school, is your consistent attendance and doing the tasks asked of you. The proof you are committed to your job or business, is that you show up daily and do the work. A good coach can do more with an average person who shows up every day willing to work, than with a talented person who shows up sporadically, who may pull off a great performance now and again. A talented athlete who is committed will achieve success in their field and will reap the rewards of that commitment.

Consistent giving of our time, talents/skills and resources, are an outward expression of our heart condition, but it is also important to note, it is not just about what you give, but how you give.
It is possible to give grudgingly, where you are reluctant or give out of obligation or duress. As much as people think, "well, at least I did it", or "at least I gave it", they need to understand that *how* they give tells a lot about whether they really care. The beginning of the Love chapter clearly states that, you can do all the "right things" and still miss it, because you didn't really care. You did not love.

Though I speak with the tongues of men and of angels, but have not love, I have become sounding brass or a clanging cymbal. And though I have the gift of prophecy, and understand all mysteries and all knowledge, and though I have all faith, so that I could remove mountains, but have not love, I am nothing. And though I bestow all my goods to feed the poor, and though I give my body to be burned, but have not love, it profits me nothing. 1 Corinthians 13:1-3

You can make the ultimate sacrifice, but if your motives weren't genuine, God does not recognise it.

But the Lord weighs and examines the hearts [of people and their motives]. Proverbs 21:2 (AMP)

In the story of Cain and Abel, God was displeased with Cain's sacrifice and rejected it. This led Cain to take his anger out on his brother. God saw the condition of Cains heart; he was disobedient and brought what *he* wanted to sacrifice instead of what God asked for. God asked him,

"Why are you angry? And why has your countenance fallen? If you do well, will you not be accepted? And if you do not do well, sin lies at the door. And its desire is for you, but you should rule over it." Genesis 4:6

God says that He examines the motives of the heart, and it is He who rewards and blesses according to their works. God challenged Cain to take stock of himself and repent. Though sin lies in wait as a lion ready to devour, nevertheless, he had the power to overcome it. We all have a choice. Regardless of circumstances and influences, we always have a choice. You can change your heart and mind at any time by the grace of God. No state is permanent, and change begins with a different choice. Cain could have chosen to heed God's words and repent. He could have started afresh with God, right then and there. Instead, he chose anger and killed his brother. God in his love and mercy will always provide opportunities to change; to make a different decision or choose a different path. He is trying to save you and restore you. If you know He is speaking to you about change and a different path, take the opportunity.

I have set before you life and death, blessing and cursing. Therefore, choose life, that both you and your descendants may live. Deuteronomy 30:19

We might be able to fool people for a time, but our fruit will ultimately give us away.

Do not be deceived, God is not mocked; for whatever a man sows, that he will also reap. Galatians 6:7

God can never be fooled by our works, so it is up to us by His Grace, to maintain a clean heart and pure motives. When we do, even if people don't appreciate it or reject it, God will respect our heart and sacrifice and will reward us accordingly.

How do we give to God?

1. Obedience
Our obedience is the first and most important thing we can give to God. When He calls, answer. When he asks, do. When He commands, harken.

If you love me, keep my commandments. John 14:15

2. <u>Time</u>
Give him your time. Spend time in the Word (God is His Word so when you read it you are with Him) and in Prayer (regular communication with Him, speaking as well as listening). Adam walked and talked with God in the Garden. Some of the most profound things that happened in the Bible came during, or because of a conversation with God.

Also, give your time in service of others and the Kingdom. Helping your family or neighbours, and serving in your church, and volunteering. God's heart is for His people, and if we love God, we must love His people.

So, when they had eaten breakfast, Jesus said to Simon Peter, "Simon, son of Jonah, do you love Me more than these?"
He said to Him, "Yes, Lord; You know that I love You." He said to him, "Feed My lambs." He said to him again a second time, "Simon, son of Jonah, do you love Me?" He said to Him, "Yes, Lord; You know that I love You." He said to him, "Tend My sheep."
He said to him the third time, "Simon, son of Jonah, do you love Me?" Peter was grieved because He said to him the third time, "Do you love Me?" And he said to Him, "Lord, you know all things; You know that I love You." Jesus said to him, "Feed My sheep.
John 21:15-17

3. Talents/Skills
We must use our gifts in gratitude to the Giver, to be a conduit for His glory. We are commanded to go into the world and make disciples of nations. Our gifts and talents were given to aid this calling. We must communicate God's love, goodness and judgement by all the means at our disposal and use those same gifts to continue to edify and encourage the Body of Christ. We all have a calling in the Kingdom of God; the purpose for which God made us and sent us into this world. You may be called to be a Father, Leader, Teacher, Mother, Artist, Builder etc. Your gifts are

given to aid the calling on your life.

And Moses said to the children of Israel, "See, the Lord has called by name Bezalel the son of Uri, the son of Hur, of the tribe of Judah; and He has filled him with the Spirit of God, in wisdom and understanding, in knowledge and all manner of workmanship, to design artistic works, to work in gold and silver and bronze, in cutting jewels for setting, in carving wood, and to work in all manner of artistic workmanship.
Exodus 35: 30-33

Bezalel was called by God to build and furnish the tabernacle. He was a gifted craftsman who was skilled with a variety of mediums. God blessed him with knowledge and wisdom to fulfil his purpose, crafting and furnishing the place of worship.
As you use your gifts in service to others, you are fulfilling your purpose while developing your gifts and turning them into skills. There is a saying that "Whatever you don't use, you lose." When we don't use our gifts, we risk losing them, and the bible illustrates this in the parable of the talents.
Jesus said:

For the kingdom of heaven is like a man traveling to a far country, who called his own servants and delivered his goods to them. And to one he gave five talents, to another two, and to another one, to each according to his own ability; and immediately he went on a journey. Then he who had received the five talents went and traded with them and made another five talents. And likewise, he who had received two gained two more also. But he who had received one went and dug in the ground and hid his lord's money. After a long time, the lord of those servants came and settled accounts with them.

"So, he who had received five talents came and brought five other talents, saying, 'Lord, you delivered to me five talents; look, I have gained five more talents besides them.' His lord said to him, 'Well done, good and faithful servant; you were faithful over a few things, I will make you ruler over many things. Enter the joy of your lord.' He also who had received two talents came and said, 'Lord, you delivered to me two talents; look, I have gained two more talents besides them.' His lord said to him, 'Well done, good and faithful servant; you have been faithful over a few things, I will make you ruler over many things. Enter the joy of your lord.'

"Then he who had received the one talent came and said, 'Lord, I knew you to be a hard man, reaping where you have not sown, and gathering where you have not scattered seed. And I was afraid and went and hid your talent in the ground. Look, there you have what is yours.'

"But his lord answered and said to him, 'You wicked and lazy servant, you knew that I reap where I have not sown and gather where I have not scattered seed. So, you ought to have deposited my money with the bankers, and at my coming I would have received back my own with interest. So, take the talent from him and give it to him who has ten talents.

'For to everyone who has, more will be given, and he will have abundance; but from him who does not have, even what he has will be taken away. And cast the

unprofitable servant into the outer darkness.
Matthew 25:14-30

God wastes nothing! Whether you have one or ten gifts, you have more than enough to do great exploits for God and have lasting impact. Jesus said, those who hide or don't use their gifts are "wicked and lazy", and what they've been given will be taken away. The "Master" continues to say that, at the very least, the servant could have deposited it in the bank, so that he could at least get some interest on His money. This was very interesting to me. As we know, Jesus used parables, or stories to teach lessons or communicate mysteries so the disciples could understand. I meditated on this and asked God about this part of the text. The thought came, if the parallel is that Jesus is the 'master' and the 'servants' are you and I, then what if the 'bank' is 'the church'. Our gift and talents are to be used to benefit and bless the world, but if for whatever reason we can't or don't go into the world, or use our gifts in the Marketplace, then at the very least, we can use our talents in our local church. The servant instead decided to hide his talent altogether, and the master received no return on his investment. We know, like the servant knew, we will all have to give a full accounting of our lives when Jesus returns, and He will expect to find us profitable and actively using the gifts and talents he died to secure for us. No more excuses! There is no reason not to use what we have been given. Even in its lowest capacity, our gifts can bring glory to God. Sometimes our condition in life is a result of our failure to be who we are and use what we have. God asked Moses, "What is in your hand?"

What do *you* have that you don't see as anything. Even the smallest gift can have big impact if you are willing to trust God and move! The thing you despise could very well be the seed that will produce your greatest blessing.

Our gifts are part of us, and by serving and ministering to others, we are giving of ourselves, and if Christ be in us, we are sharing Him also. We are God's hands in the earth, vessels of honour and conduits for his love and blessing to the world.

4. Resources

Our resources are our tangible material goods. Tithing and regular giving to your church demonstrates your commitment to your church. We invest in our homes to ensure it has all the necessities, decorations and furnishings to make it comfortable, and provide security and peace. Our homes serve a specific purpose and are designed according to what we need, that's why no two homes are alike. Our homes need to be maintained. There are bills, repairs, insurance etc, regular expenses to maintain your home. In the same way, we must build and maintain the sanctuary of God in the earth. Furnish and decorate so it is comfortable, secure and peaceful. What is your reaction when you go to someone's house, and it is out of order? How then do you think the people would react upon visiting your church and encountering disorder? Remember, these are the people we are trying to make into disciples.

God says we must build him a house where he can put his name. A place of worship where an altar is established to offer sacrifices, praise and thanksgiving, and a point of divine exchange between heaven and earth. A storehouse where people can run to and remain until he returns to gather His harvest.

"Heaven is My throne, and earth is My footstool. Where is the house that you will build Me? And where is the place of My rest? Isaiah 66:1

Then all the congregation of the people of Israel departed from the presence of Moses. And they came, everyone whose heart stirred him, and everyone whose spirit moved him, and brought the Lord's contribution to be used for the tent of meeting, and for all its service, and for the holy garments. So, they came, both men and women. All who were of a willing heart brought brooches and earrings and signet rings and armlets, all sorts of gold objects, every man dedicating an offering of gold to the Lord.
Exodus 35:20-22 ESV

After the Israelites were delivered from slavery, God led them to the wilderness and commissioned a tabernacle for worship. He commanded the people to bring their resources to help build and furnish it. The instructions to the people are detailed in Exodus 35; the following highlighted verses are God's instruction to the people.

Take from among you an offering to the Lord. Whoever is of a willing heart, let him bring it as an offering to the Lord... Exodus 35:5

All who are gifted artisans among you shall come and make all that the Lord has commanded: the tabernacle, its tent, its covering, its clasps, its boards, its bars, its pillars, and its sockets…. Exodus 35:10-11

*Then everyone came whose heart was stirred, and everyone whose spirit was willing, and they brought the Lord's offering for the work of the tabernacle of meeting, for all its service, and for the holy garments. They came, both men and women, as many as had a willing heart, and brought earrings and nose rings, rings and necklaces, all jewellery of gold, that is, every man who made an offering of gold to the Lord.
Exodus 35:21-22*

God gave the children of Israel the responsibility of providing the resources required for building the tabernacle. When God delivered the Israelites out of Egypt, they were extremely wealthy. After the plagues, the Egyptians realised they would be cursed if the Israelites stayed there. The Egyptians compelled them to leave and gave them their wealth and anything they could carry so they would leave quickly.

*Then he called for Moses and Aaron by night, and said, "Rise, go out from among my people, both you and the children of Israel. And go, serve the Lord as you have said. Also take your flocks and your herds, as you have said, and be gone; and bless me also."
And the Egyptians urged the people, that they might send them out of the land in haste. For they said, "We shall all be dead." So, the people took their dough before it was leavened, having their kneading bowls*

bound up in their clothes on their shoulders. Now the children of Israel had done according to the word of Moses, and they had asked from the Egyptians articles of silver, articles of gold, and clothing. And the Lord had given the people favour in the sight of the Egyptians, so that they granted them what they requested. Thus, they plundered the Egyptians.
Exodus 12:31-36

The instructions and method for the tabernacle were given to Moses, but the means to build and maintain it was given to the people. We are blessed to be a blessing to our church and community.

Minister

Before the word 'minister' was a noun, it was a verb, and it means 'to attend to the needs of someone'. The word was used to refer to a doctor, nurse or someone who provided care for the sick. In Latin, the word translates as 'servant'. We either minister to God, or minister to people.

You shall anoint them, consecrate them, and sanctify them, that they may minister to Me as priests.
Exodus 28:41

Some of us are called to minister before God as priests, i.e., intermediaries between God and the people. These intercessors stand before God to lead the people in worship and prayer or to stand in the gap on their behalf.

They were ministering with music before the dwelling place of the tabernacle of meeting, until Solomon had built the house of the Lord in Jerusalem, and they served in their office according to their order.
1 Chronicles 6:32

Jesus came to us as a servant, and His life was ministry to the world, but he also needed to be ministered to. For example, the woman with the alabaster box, and at His death, we also learn of the women who ministered to, and supported Him.

"There were also women looking on from afar, among whom were Mary Magdalene, Mary the mother of James the Less and of Joses, and Salome, who also followed Him and ministered to Him when He was in Galilee, and many other women who came up with Him to Jerusalem". Mark 15:40-41

In Matthew chapter four, after his temptation, the bible says that after Jesus passed the test, angels came and ministered to Him. The verse does not state how the angels ministered to Jesus, but in the book of Daniel, we have an example of the ministry of angels. In Daniel 10, the prophet recounts his period of mourning and fasting. The angel, after being resisted three weeks came in answer to Daniels prayer, but he was weakened from the fast and could not stand. It then says in verse 18, that the angel touched him and strengthened Him.

God calls all His children, and Jesus commanded His followers, to go into the world and make disciples. We are charged to do greater works, in fact, He promises that we will. We have a calling to minister to others in any way we can, using our gifts, talents and resources.

"A new commandment I give to you; that you love one another; as I have loved you, that you also love one another." John 13:34

Every person we meet is an opportunity to share the love of God or meet a need.

His Love, Not Your Deeds

God doesn't love you because of what you do, he loves you because it is who *He* is.

I began to meditate on the apocalyptic events in the bible, and I concluded that the first one should have been the only one. In the book of Genesis, we read that God destroyed the world by The Flood, and saved Noah's family to begin again.

Then the Lord saw that the wickedness of man was great in the earth, and that every intent of the thoughts of his heart was only evil continually. And the Lord was sorry that He had made man on the earth, and He was grieved in His heart. So, the Lord said, "I will destroy man whom I have created from the face of the earth, both man and beast, creeping thing and birds of the air, for I am sorry that I have made them." But Noah found grace in the eyes of the Lord.
Genesis 6:5-8

Despite this, men continued to sin, and wickedness

once again grew in the earth. Since the flood, apocalyptic destructions were localised. For example, the wonders in Egypt, Sodom and Gomorrah; but nothing on the planetary scale of the flood. It hasn't happened, but it is written, that God *will* make a new heaven and a new earth, and this one will pass away.

He who was seated on the throne said, "I am making everything new!" Then he said, "Write this down, for these words are trustworthy and true."
Revelation 21:5 (NIV)

God's love for us, prevents him from destroying the world, but ultimately, His love will compel him to act, so sin and evil will be eradicated permanently. Whether you believe in creationism or evolution, that we have been here for a few thousand years, or other scientific theories that place us here millions of years ago, either way, we have been here a long time. God's patience is unfathomable. We have had a long time to repent, choose him, and choose holiness.

Please know that nothing written here is meant to generate fear or doubt. This book is meant to uplift and inspire you and be a source of encouragement to your life. Don't be anxious and worried about living up to religious expectations, or a man-made ideal of what it is to be a child of God. Maintain constant contact with God through prayer and stay in the Word. Develop intimacy with God and take it one day at a time. Never condemn yourself when you make mistakes. Mistakes mean you are moving and growing. There is nothing you can do that will stop God from loving you. There's nothing that you did that will stop

God from loving you. If you do good, He loves you; if you don't, He still loves you, because His love is not dependent on your acts or your behaviour. His love depends only on him. He cannot hate you because He is love. The things that God hates are listed in Proverbs, and you and I aren't there! It lists behaviours not people. He tells us what He hates, to help us recognise when we have stumbled out of righteousness so we can correct it. By this, we will know His mind and understand Him more.

The more I know about my friends, their likes and dislikes, the closer I am to them. There's nothing better than being known by the people you care about. There's a level of security and safety within the relationship because you have understanding and know what they will and won't do. Jesus said, "My sheep know my voice." To get to know God's voice, we must develop intimacy with Him, beginning with spending time in His Word. God called Abraham his friend, and David a man after his own heart. Intimacy is very important to God, but you can't achieve intimacy if you're always fearful of Him. God communicates his perfect love daily through his word. So, get stuck in and get to know Him. Believe that neither death, hell, the grave, your attitude, your behaviour, your thoughts, your friends, circumstance, bad decisions, absolutely nothing can separate you from His Love.

LOVING YOURSELF

As You Love Yourself...

You shall love the LORD your God with all your heart, with all your soul, and with all your mind.' And the second is like it: 'You shall love your neighbour as yourself. Matthew 22:37-40

The order is, Love God, then yourself, so you can love others. We must have our love priorities in order! God is first. We are commanded to love Him with our entire being and with everything we have. Then we are commanded to love others, as we love ourselves. Both God and Jesus during His time on earth said the same thing and dubbed it the greatest commandment. God says, if you can do that, you've fulfilled the entire law. Isn't God good? He loves us so much he simplified righteousness. If we obey this commandment, we may come to him freely and live a holy life in right-standing with Him. He says, 'Love Me, and as you love yourself, love others.' When you love God with all your heart, when Jesus is Lord of your life, and when you have submitted to the guidance and teaching of the Holy spirit, your being will be flooded with His love. You will 'see' and 'know' God, and by the same token will 'see' and 'know' yourself. Subsequently, as you embrace and walk in His love every day, you will love yourself and others as He commands.

The Priority Pyramid

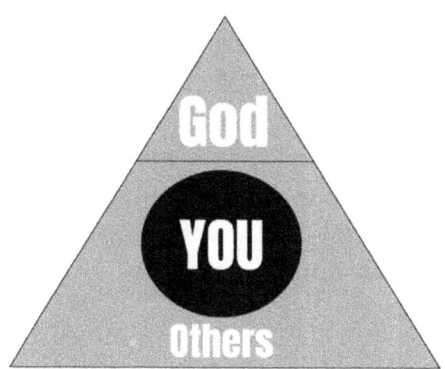

Please note, that loving yourself or others is neither higher nor lower in priority; they are both equally important in relation to each other. Though the pyramid is illustrated with multiple sections, it is one. One principle, one love.

You cannot fully receive the love of God and hate yourself. It's impossible! You cannot love others if you hate yourself, and you cannot hate others and say that you love God.

Whoever claims to love God yet hates a brother or sister is a liar. For whoever does not love their brother and sister, whom they have seen, cannot love God, whom they have not seen. 1 John 4:20 (NIV)

When you come to know the love of God, you will begin to understand God's heart, His mind, and His thoughts towards you. He wants the best for you; He strengthens empowers and guides you. He loves you always, even before you were born, and His plan is to give you everything He is, and everything He has. You are a jewel in His crown, fearfully and wonderfully made; a work of art, sculpted, moulded and created by the One and only God of the universe. Once you realise how much God loves you and why, it will change the way you feel about yourself. If you love God, how can you despise yourself or mistreat yourself knowing the great value He has placed on you, and in you?

Beware of Pride!
Self-love must always be tempered by the Word of God. Otherwise, if we are not vigilant, it may turn into selfishness, pride, or worse, narcissism. We are humans and we won't get it right all the time, but if we obey the first commandment, there is always forgiveness and a way back into right standing with God.

Pride is all about protecting 'self' to the exclusion of God. For example, we may understand on the surface that God loves and knows everything about us, but still take this 'grace' for granted. We convince ourselves that because God hasn't "struck us down" we can't be "that bad". We go about our lives for a time believing everything is good until God's correction comes. Maybe we start a new Bible reading plan, or your Pastor starts a new teaching series, or you start watching Christian television, but as you hear the word of God, which is like a spiritual mirror, the conviction of the Holy Spirit opens your understanding to recognise that you have fallen short. What then do you do? A Prideful person would withdraw immediately from God and His word, anticipating the hurt and shame from owning and admitting their failings. They wish to avoid the discomfort of repentance, and tell themselves they're ok, after all they are 'not as bad as some people.' They lack the courage to face the reality of their true state or nature and try to cover it. In the same way, Adam and Eve who were originally 'naked' before God and had no secrets, tried to cover themselves after they sinned in the Garden. They knew they were wrong and tried to cover their shame with leaves, and by lying and blaming each other. Humility says, "I will trust God;" no matter what comes to the surface, it is met with prayer and thanksgiving, and full confidence in a loving Father who reveals to redeem. This is the faith we must have in God.

Pride is also having confidence and trust in your own efforts and achievements while actively bolstering your reputation. God loved David, and David loved God with is whole heart, but in selfishness, David coveted another man's wife and took her, then in his pride, orchestrated the death of the woman's husband, and if that wasn't bad enough, he numbered the people against God's instructions to keep the charade going. Pride is very dangerous, as it usually will do everything it can to maintain its existence and cover up failings. David was wrong, but he tried to protect his reputation and his self-worth by covering His wrong. Another symptom of pride is self-reliance, having no need for God, His help or His forgiveness. But without faith it is impossible to please God, and He was not pleased with David's actions. David should have trusted that God loved him (which he did in the end), confessed his weakness and asked God for help from the outset, but he let his actions take root and grow into murder and obstruction of justice. The consequences of King David's decisions were ultimately very costly both to him and to the people. The good news is that despite his failings, once he humbled himself, God forgave and restored him. David, son of Jesse was Israel's greatest king, not because of what he did, but because he obeyed the greatest commandment, and God declared him 'a man after his own heart'. The story of David gives us hope that God can and will forgive any wrong if we ask Him, as long as we have a humble heart.

Loving Me

Be Honest
Endeavour to speak the truth to, and about yourself always, and you will do the same for others. Being honest with yourself is one of the hardest things you will do, but it is a necessary exercise in humility. To be truly humble is to come face to face with who you are and face your true thoughts, your fears and your actions. I stated earlier in the book that we are our own worst critic, and as such, we tend to fear the level of vulnerability it takes to be brutally honest with ourselves. Where we are talented, strong and excellent, we also tend to fear coming across arrogant or boastful, so we try to make ourselves small in the eyes of others. It is ok to know you are worthy,

powerful and strong, and to be your whole self every day. Who you are will show; you don't need to say a word. Knowing who you are makes you confident, resilient and humble; knowledge of oneself is a shield from negative words, that will also help you to recover quickly from life's difficulties.

We must also be honest about our motives. We would like to think that we have pure motives, but we must be honest. Why are you doing that thing? Why did you say that. No one is immune to selfishness. In the moment, it is not easy to identify, in fact, it is usually after reflection that we recognise our true intentions in a particular circumstance, and it can be difficult to own. But recognising it and changing our behaviour is good growth and maturity.

Loving yourself, means not lying to yourself. We sometimes endure and stay in situations that are slowly killing us spiritually and emotionally, and we convince ourselves we are doing the right thing, but in truth, it is because we fear the alternative or the unknown. God will always back-up the truth. There is a peace and freedom that comes with truthfulness. Much of our anxiety comes from a lack of truth and ignorance of the facts. Be honest! Love rejoices in the truth, and Jesus said:

If you abide in My word, then you are my disciples indeed, and you shall know the truth, and the truth shall set you free. John 8:31-32

We must always take the time, wherever possible, to both celebrate the positives and identify and correct

and deal with the negatives, and trust God with the rest. As much as it is in your control, take the time to 'nip-things-in-the-bud', lest they grow out of control and become greater problems down the road.
Be honest about who you are, your 'whole' self, and what you want. Do Not Be Afraid! God Loves you.

Forgive Yourself

Yes, you were wrong. It was the wrong choice, and you said/did it. If not for your actions, it wouldn't have happened, and you are responsible for the consequences. You did it; it's your fault.

Now what?

Now, you accept responsibility for your actions, make amends and correct what you can. Apologise, learn from it and change; forgive yourself and move on. It doesn't matter what it is, forgive yourself. No matter the opinion or conduct of others, you must! Life is life. It isn't perfect and no one is perfect. We all make mistakes and wrong choices. We can be passive at times, not making the effort or have a lazy approach to things or life in general, which consequently, impacts everyone involved negatively. We will make mistakes, both out of ignorance and wilfully. It doesn't matter how you got there, it matters how you learn from it and how you rise from it.

We now live in a world that enjoys sacrificing people on the altar of public opinion. There is a culture of unforgiveness, and now that photographic evidence can be easily stored and shared for years, people can have their mistakes revisited upon them long after the fact. But God tells us to forgive as we have been forgiven. And as many times as you have been offended, forgive. Forgive yourself as He has already forgiven you. You are worthy of forgiveness because God says He has removed your sin far from you. Why continue to condemn yourself? Would you want someone you love to live in a state of perpetual condemnation?

Don't let your mistakes hold you back from living freely. Jesus died to set you free from every sin if you believe and accept Him,

There is therefore now no condemnation to those who are in Christ Jesus, who do not walk according to the flesh, but according to the Spirit. Romans 8:1

Celebrate Yourself

Celebrate every milestone and achievement and mark them as important life occasions. Don't let birthdays, anniversaries, or accomplishments go by without recognition, even if it's just you that celebrates. This is a sign of gratitude and not only is it healthy for you, it also pleases God. It means that you do not take anything for granted, and you recognise and appreciate the blessings in your life. God gave the Israelites instructions on how and when to celebrate His goodness, and commemorate various life events, miracles and signs. He instituted these 'feasts' so the people would not forget the event. As long as you remember all the blessings in your life and all the good things that have happened and keep happening, you keep discouragement at bay. You can't be depressed and grateful at the same time. Remembering the good and celebrating keeps your mind focused on the positive rather than dwelling on the negative. We must practice gratitude. Every day is a gift, every good thing deserves acknowledgement, and every milestone and achievement should be recognised and celebrated in some way. God instituted many feasts and celebrations, and commanded the Israelites to observe them, feelings notwithstanding. Life happens, and at times it gets wearisome and drives the fight out of you. In these times, you can be so overwhelmed that it's hard to see the good. This is when you celebrate not because you feel like it, but because you must. The same David that slew Goliath and had songs sung about him was on the run from a family he loved; family who were determined to end his life, but he still honoured them. He found himself discouraged but after a while he spoke to himself. Remember the creative power of words?

Why are you cast down, O my soul?
And why are you disquieted within me?
Hope in God; For I shall yet praise Him,
The help of my countenance and my God.
Psalm 43:5

David spoke himself out of depression and followed it up with the appropriate actions. You may be discouraged and going through the thick of it and your soul is disquieted within you but have hope in God. Choose hope and remember God's goodness in your life. Praise and thank him; show Him you remember His goodness, and you are grateful. David said, "I will praise the 'help of my countenance' and my God." God is the remedy for discouragement and the cure for our countenance. In recent times the word countenance is used to describe a person's facial expression, but in this context, it refers to a person's demeanour or behaviour. Come on and celebrate!

Rest Yourself
There remains therefore a rest for the people of God. Hebrews 4:9

NOUN: THE REFRESHING QUIET OR REPOSE OF SLEEP
REFRESHING EASE OR INACTIVITY AFTER EXERTION OR LABOUR:

VERB: TO REFRESH ONESELF, AS BY SLEEPING, LYING DOWN, OR RELAXING; TO RELIEVE WEARINESS BY CESSATION OF EXERTION OR LABOUR.

VERB: (USED WITH OBJECT) TO GIVE REST TO; REFRESH WITH REST; TO REST ONESELF; TO LAY OR PLACE FOR REST, EASE, OR SUPPORT; TO BRING TO REST; HALT; STOP.

God commanded us to love Him with our entire being, our mind, heart, soul and strength, and He also commanded us to 'rest'.

Your <u>MIND</u> - cast down thoughts, overly critical or analytical, anxiety, doubt, worry, overstimulation.

Your <u>HEART</u> - emotional rest, managing ambitions, desires and expectations.

Your <u>SOUL</u> – life duties, assignment, prioritise important vs urgent, life issues (work, family pressures).

Your <u>STRENGTH</u> - your Body, physical rest striving, overwork, fatigue, overachieving, looking after your health, diet and exercise.

Rest is not a suggestion; it is a command. Humans by nature will work until they are tired. They rely on their feelings to dictate how and when they rest. Often, by the time we allow ourselves to rest, it is too late because we are already sick or exhausted. God himself rested and made it a commandment; a life principle that we should never compromise. In recent years, more research is being done to analyse and investigate the effects of sleep deprivation and the benefits of regular quality rest. These institutions are putting their resources behind these studies, why? Because we don't fully understand the effects of a lack of rest on our entire being. We are used to operating on a limited capacity, and we give ourselves trophies for pushing ahead even though we are impaired. But let's be honest, outside of temporary, urgent situations, we should take better care of ourselves. Sadly, there are also some who tend to look after possessions and pets better than themselves.

A lack of rest and restful sleep affects the body in numerous ways. These include:
- Impatience, Irritability, mood swings
- Impaired concentration and judgement
- Weakened immune system – without sufficient

rest the body cannot repair itself properly.
- Increased risk of depression and anxiety

It is hard to love when we are tired. We are more likely to be short-tempered and impatient, and the effect of the symptoms mentioned can override your best intentions. Bad choices are made when we are tired, so do your best to schedule rest and keep your mind sharp and your heart clear. Set aside time to rest in God and rest your mind and body regularly. Establish a daily routine with specific rest periods, for example, no phones after 8pm; you could also create a bedtime routine to encourage restful sleep. You could have a bath, hot drink, and read or put on relaxing music. The key is to do it daily and train your body, so as soon as you get in that bath, your body knows what time it is and starts to wind down. Also have a yearly plan; go away once or twice per year to a new environment to rest and recharge. Life will be there when you get back, but the difference will be that you are rested, clear headed and strong enough to handle it. Life's issues can be overwhelming at times and when you step back or step away, it can be very beneficial. Taking that time out allows you to view things from a different perspective, it can improve your ability to cope and refresh your problem-solving skills. Archimedes was a mathematician and scholar in ancient Greece who famously made a scientific discovery while taking a bath. Relaxation and meditation are powerful forces, the benefits of which are still being discovered.

Rest is a mystery that God commanded, and we don't

have to fully understand it before we obey. Things will arise in life that pulls us apart in one way or another, but we need to take the time to put ourselves back together. Both spiritual healing and self-healing takes time, you cannot rush it. If you remove a pie from the oven too early, the process is incomplete. Chances are it will taste horrible, no one will eat it, and you will have to find and prepare something else. It is the same when we try to rush our rest, we might feel better, but we are not rested. When life demands 100% and you only have 50%, it means you will have to borrow it from somewhere. When we over work and compromise on resting, we are borrowing from our future. We are using reserves we haven't built up yet and when we need it, it won't be there.

Life is long, we need our health to achieve our goals and see our visions and dreams come to pass. So, rest; invest in your future and make good choices now, so that you don't suffer later. The health investments you make today will sustain you in your later years.

Fight for Your Mind

Your mind can be a battlefield where brutal war is waged. The prize? Peace: it is what we all want – to be at peace with ourselves and others and exist in a state of satisfaction and joy. It is sometimes thought that peace is the absence of strife or difficulty, in fact, God says we can have peace at any time and in all circumstances. John 14:27 says,

My peace I leave with you, My peace I give to you; not as the world gives do I give to you.

Peace is a fruit of the spirit that can be cultivated. God says this is what identifies you as His child. Matthew 5:6 says,

Blessed are the peacemakers, for they shall be called sons of God.

Peace of mind is very hard to achieve because anxiety is almost a reflex action, not to mention we live in a society where there are various triggers, which increase daily; but God has given instructions about how to rest and when.

For the weapons of our warfare are not carnal but mighty in God for pulling down strongholds, casting down arguments and every high thing that exalts itself against the knowledge of God, bringing every thought into captivity to the obedience of Christ and being ready to punish all disobedience when your obedience is fulfilled. 2 Corinthians 10:4-6

God says renew your mind with His; take hold and meditate on His promises, instructions and wisdom, then eliminate and dispose of every thought that rises in opposition to the truth you 'know' in your heart. Most believers are overwhelmed by negative thoughts because they don't have enough revelation and understanding of God's Word. The sword of the Spirit which is the word of God is the only 'Offensive' weapon in the Armour of God, but it is all you need. The rest are defensive; spiritual armour to protect your mind and body, but we are not just to be defensive. We also have the means to attack! When I meditate on, "*casting down arguments and every high thing that exalts itself against the knowledge of God,*" I visualise that my mind is a private place with 'heavy set, muscular security personnel guarding its doors. They only give entry to visitors who were invited and whose name is found on the list, or in the book. Anyone else is refused entry because they don't belong there, and should they persist, the security has power and authority to use force to remove them from the premises. This is what I visualise when the scripture says, 'Cast down'. When those negative thoughts and ideas come, whether from within or external sources, don't invite them in for 'tea' and entertain them, but promptly and forcibly wrestle each and every one of them to the ground and throw them out! Do whatever you must so it doesn't take root; remove yourself from the environment and take charge of your atmosphere. Also speak! Do not be silent; praise God, speak the opposite, speak what God says out loud and go on the attack, because like we said earlier, peace is difficult to obtain, and you must fight for it.

There Is Only One Saviour

The Bible story about the woman with the issue of blood speaks about her drawing her healing out of Jesus. Her faith prompted an involuntary response of healing from the Lord.

Now a certain woman had a flow of blood for twelve years and had suffered many things from many physicians. She had spent all that she had and was no better, but rather grew worse. When she heard about

Jesus, she came behind Him in the crowd and touched His garment. For she said, "If only I may touch His clothes, I shall be made well." Immediately the fountain of her blood was dried up, and she felt in her body that she was healed of the affliction. And Jesus, immediately knowing in Himself that power had gone out of Him, turned around in the crowd and said, "Who touched My clothes?" But His disciples said to Him, "You see the multitude thronging You, and You say, 'Who touched Me?'" And He looked around to see her who had done this thing. But the woman, fearing and trembling, knowing what had happened to her, came and fell down before Him and told Him the whole truth. And He said to her, "Daughter, your faith has made you well. Go in peace and be healed of your affliction."

Jesus asked the question because he felt the power leave Him. He then told the woman her faith made her well. What can we learn from this? People can draw virtue from you. We are spiritual beings first, so once there is connection, physical, emotional or soul-ties, people can draw from you. Jesus was connected to the people emotionally through compassion, the woman connected to Him physically by touch, and spiritually by faith. The Son of God had power, but even He, at times had to withdraw to recharge and replenish, how much more then, you or I? People can draw from us to feed their needs and will deplete our emotional resources if we're not careful. If Jesus allowed the people constant access and they continually drew from Him, he probably wouldn't have completed His mission due to sheer exhaustion. I admonish you brethren, love people, have compassion and help wherever and whenever you can, but you are not their Saviour, and you must learn when and how to say No. Take time regularly to replenish yourself and do not compromise your God-Time! You are no good to anyone without it.

Advocate for Yourself

Set Healthy Boundaries!
When you set boundaries, it will attract criticism, particularly from those who enjoyed the benefits of unlimited access. Don't let this deter you! There are times we must be vulnerable for the greater good, and in those times, we operate by faith in our loving Father. The only person who has an all-access pass is God. Then your spouse, because the 'two' is one. This is why you must be careful who you marry as you are bonded soul and spirit.

Jesus was very present during His ministry, but he maintained healthy boundaries and gave different levels of access to different people. John 2:24 says that He did not 'entrust' Himself to people because He knew their hearts. People may mean well, and some may have the best intentions, but they still could potentially be a stumbling block to you. Follow our Lord's example and protect yourself. Speak up when you need to, and do not be afraid to make determinations for yourself. Not rudely but be assertive! Only you determine the amount of power a person can have over you.

Speak Over Yourself

Death and life are in the power of the tongue: and they that love it shall eat the fruit thereof.
Proverbs 18:21(KJV)

God says, you will have whatever you say. Never underestimate the power of positive confession! Speaking is a 'creative' power that God gave to mankind. Once you say a thing, the universe immediately reacts and manipulates reality to bring what you've said into being. We have the power to change and shape our lives and determine our success or failure by the words we speak. This practice has been a well-kept secret of successful people for centuries, but it is a God-idea, and a gift He also shared with us. God *spoke* the world into existence, and he only 'spoke' the things He wanted to create.

Then God said, "Let there be light"; and there was light. And God saw the light, that it was good...
Genesis 1:3-4

Instead of stating the obvious and affirming the darkness, He spoke the solution, the thing he wanted, and "there was light." Not only did it come to pass but God saw that "it was good." It is good to speak positively about yourself and make declarations based on God's promises to you, and regarding your dreams and goals. It is ok to hold yourself in good regard and a level of esteem, but it must be tempered with the Word of God.

For I say, through the grace given to me, to everyone who is among you, not to think of himself more highly than he ought to think, but to think soberly, as God has dealt to each one a measure of faith. Romans 12:3

God also says, we must guard our hearts because everything flows from it. He warns us in the scriptures about how to deal with pain and hurt, and then instructs us on how we should conduct ourselves in difficult situations. Difficult times are opportunities for the adversary to plant seeds of bitterness and discouragement in our lives. If we allow it, we will make negative confessions and act from a place of sorrow instead of faith. God says:

There is a time to weep, and a time to laugh; a time to mourn, and a time to dance… Ecclesiastes 3:4

…do not let the sun go down on your wrath… Ephesians 4:26

Its ok to be angry, but not for more than a day. Its ok to mourn, but not more than the "mourning period". After that, you will be in danger of seeding bitterness and discouragement in your heart. BE VIGILANT! Everything has a time, and a 'time limit'. Negativity is the product, or a symptom of a bitter heart, but God is the remedy!

Finally, brethren, whatsoever things are true, whatsoever things are honest, whatsoever things are just, whatsoever things are pure, whatsoever things are lovely, whatsoever things are of good report; if there be any virtue, and if there be any praise, think on these things. Philippians 4:8 (KJV)

Whatever you focus on will grow, that is a fact. Focusing on good things will bring joy, and this will give you the strength you need to hold-fast and persevere. This does not mean that you ignore difficulties hoping they will disappear. It means that despite the difficulty, you maintain your joy and objectivity with your heart intact, so you can endure and overcome.

Here are a few confessions to get started:

Building Your Faith
I am loved
I am the righteousness of God in Christ
I am redeemed
I will not fear
I am forgiven
I am healed
I have the mind of Christ
I am more than a conqueror
I am not alone I am blessed

Building your Self-Esteem
I am beautiful
I am worthy
I am success, so I will succeed
I speak life over myself always
I will prosper
I am hopeful
I am a giver
I am more than able

I am capable
I am more than enough
I am not perfect, but I'm loved by the One who is

<u>Mind Your Words</u>
God also wants us to be careful of idle, thoughtless words. Speaking without giving thought or care to what we say, still has impact. We may not realise it in the moment, but God says we will give an account of EVERY word we speak or have spoken.

But I say to you that for every idle word that men may speak; they will give account of it in the day of judgment. Matthew 12:36

There are times when it will be difficult to mind our words, especially when emotions are high. This is why self-control is so important. God's words are powerful because He doesn't speak idly. He doesn't speak for speaking sake. Every word has a purpose and is written to accomplish just that. He doesn't waste words, nor does He make fake promises or empty threats; when He speaks, it is done, and so must our words be.

So shall My word be that goes forth from My mouth; It shall not return to Me void, but it shall accomplish what I please, and it shall prosper in the thing for which I sent it. Isaiah 55:11

If we practice dishonesty, we won't believe our own confessions. That's why it's important to love God and yourself enough to practice honesty, so that when we speak, it has weight. God wants us to take care and

Develop Yourself

Whatever you can't do, learn to do; anything you can do, learn to do it better. Whenever possible, take full advantage of every opportunity to improve your strengths and skills. The greatest and largest room is the 'room for improvement'. You will never get to a place where you know or can do it all. There is always room to grow. Regardless of where you are now, there is a higher level. Self-improvement must never stem from abuse or rooted in fear or pride. There are people who drive themselves mentally and physically, striving to live up to an ideal, or the expectation of others. When we are honest with ourselves, and we allow the Holy Spirit to guide us, we will learn to balance contentment with ambition.

GOD, GRANT ME THE SERENITY TO ACCEPT THE THINGS I CANNOT CHANGE, THE COURAGE TO CHANGE THE THINGS I CAN AND THE WISDOM TO KNOW THE DIFFERENCE.

There are somethings that only God can do, and we must trust Him to do so. This is why knowing Him is so important.
We need to grow and evolve, otherwise are we even living?

I can do all things through Christ who strengthens me. Philippians 4:13

These are a few lessons I've learned over the years and use as quotes to motivate myself.

- Always give something new a try.
- Test yourself and stretch your limits.
- Comfort and contentment are not always the same thing.
- You won't necessarily know you are in your comfort zone until you leave it.
- People are people and they will do what they will do; the only thing in your control is what YOU say and do.
- Be willing to try anything once and 'know you can't do or like something, rather than assume off the bat that you can't, or don't.
- Knowledge is good, but understanding is better. Wisdom is power.
- Sometimes you must take a leap of faith, or you'll die in the comfort zone.
- You were born alone, and you will die alone, so be bold and do things on your own.
- Help doesn't mean you are incapable; it just means you need help.
- Yesterday's you expired, yesterday.
- You have everything you need, to do everything you need to do.
- The answer to your issue is already there, waiting for you to discover it.
- Sometimes your dilemma is a struggle between what you want to do and what can be done.
- Sometimes you must follow your heart or go with your gut; other times you must calculate the risk and work the problem like a mathematician.

Check Yourself

Most people wait until something goes wrong before they do any maintenance, whether it be an object or relationship. Do you wait until the car breaks down before you take it to the garage? Do you wait until your teeth hurt before you visit the dentist? Bishop taught us a while ago that, "it is better to build a fence at the top of the cliff, than a hospital at the bottom." My clever brain would add, "you should probably do both because being what they are, human beings would still somehow find themselves over the edge." Nevertheless, the principle is sound, 'prevention is better than cure.' We can incur painful losses when we fail to realise and take responsibility for our actions. It takes two to tango and there are three sides to every story, your side, my side and the truth. All sides must face the truth and agree with the truth if there is to be healing and forgiveness. Must you lose your friends and family before you check yourself and realise that you were part of the problem? The truth is neutral; it is not a respecter of persons, and it cannot be bent to the will of the individual, in fact, the individual must submit to it.

Search me O God, and know my heart; try me and know my anxieties. See if there is any wicked way in me, and lead me in the way everlasting.
Psalm 139:23-24

LOVING OTHERS

Love thy Neighbour!

By this all will know that you are My disciples, if you have love for one another. John 13:34-35

In the previous chapters, we discussed what love is, ways of loving God and loving ourselves. Woven within the text we also learned the characteristics of love and how to treat others. Now that we understand a bit more, we must now take those lessons and apply it daily in loving others, and with the same care and determination we have for ourselves. The Agape love: that brotherly love and regard for human life, is what God wants and is the evidence of a thriving, stable society. The first five commandments in Exodus 20 begin with our relations with God and then our families, but the final five are specifically about how we treat and exist with others.

"You shall not murder".

"You shall not commit adultery.

"You shall not steal.

"You shall not bear false witness against your neighbour.

"You shall not covet your neighbour's house; you shall not covet your neighbour's wife, nor his male servant, nor his female servant, nor his ox, nor his donkey, nor anything that is your neighbour's." Exodus 20:13-17

The rest of the law given in Leviticus is an expansion of these. You would not want to be treated unjustly, inhumanely or be a victim of theft or assault. You would demand what is right, fair and just for you and your family, so God says, do the same for others.

And just as you want men to do to you, you also do to them likewise. Luke 6:31

God loves people, and we are the tools and vessels He uses to show that love. However, if we do not love others, He cannot use us to accomplish His purpose, because we will resist Him. We will let our emotions and feelings about people get in the way of God's will. It is not easy to show kindness to someone who has hurt you or give to someone who has taken from you. This is why you must receive God's love first and get to know Him, only then will you see people through His eyes, and in so doing, you will develop the ability to separate your hurt from the person and what God is asking of you. In the book of Genesis, God admonished us to subdue and have dominion in the earth. This was a command to every person, and in obedience we must have dominion, all of us together. Over the centuries however, we have seen that men have only striven to subdue and have dominion over each other. If only we could correct this error! This is not a job for one person. The world is vast, and being concerned with the welfare of billions is too much for one person alone. If, however, we can all work together to obey this one commandment and love our neighbour, this small act can affect real change, eventually leading to a world filled with hope.

How does God ask us to love others?
1. Feed My Lambs, Tend My Sheep, Feed my Sheep

Jesus told Peter, if you love Me, you will do these three things.

a) Feed my Lamb – Lambs are young and cannot look after themselves. They need to be fed, nourished and supervised until they can fend for themselves. Wherever we can, we should look after those who need it. Jesus taught us to pray, 'Give us this day our daily bread'. We ask God for the food or sustenance we need, but when the bread, or the means to acquire it is in our capability, God says we should help where we can. To feed and nurture people takes patience and a genuine regard for others.

b) Tend My Sheep – God says be there for people when you can. The word 'tend' means to 'care for', 'take care of' or 'attend to'. Your presence is valuable and is always appreciated. Christians hunger for God's presence because there is a profound peace in knowing that you are not alone, and God is with you in everything. In life and particularly in difficult situations, having someone there is the difference between life and death, loss and victory, success and failure. We were not made to be alone, and we were not meant to fight battles alone. There is strength in numbers. God has created and orchestrated life where we need each other. No man is an island, and we need people to flourish and thrive.

We are here because of relationships. Relationships give meaning and drives purpose. The relationships we have, the experiences, the connections and the interactions can be motivating, inspiring and satisfying. Love is omnidirectional; it flows out like waves, but it also flows in, in just the same way. We read earlier that Agape is robust and has great capacity, but it is up to us to let that love flow without fear, because we know that it is God's love flowing through us, and we are both conduits and beneficiaries.

Building A Community In Love
Above all clothe yourselves with love, which binds us all together in perfect harmony. Colossians 3:14

Facing the Extreme
We are aware of the wickedness and destruction that mankind is capable of. We see it in the news every day, and some of us have first-hand experience. At the time of writing this section, a terrible crime occurred in our city where a fourteen-year-old boy was killed on his way to school, and a few others seriously injured by a man who got up one morning intent on hurting everyone in his path. We do not know why, and as a society which always tries to understand why things happen, it is heart wrenching when there is no real reason, and the loss of life is senseless. The public reaction to the incident was sadness, but there was also rage. Rage against a person who committed this awful act, and understandably so. Some called for the death penalty others wish the most heinous punishments upon him. But I ask you to stop and think for a moment about that man. Does he deserve love? Should he be shown compassion?

What would Jesus do? Justice and compassion are not the same thing, and they cannot cancel each other out. If you commit a crime, you should be tried, and sentenced. But while in prison, should you be deprived of food, or the basic needs of a human being? Should you be beaten and mistreated because you have done this thing, and everyone believes you deserve no less than the act you committed? Meditate on these questions and compare them with the scriptures you have read in this book. What do you think?

Loving others is not an easy thing. At times it requires real sacrifice and a strong will, because your natural response will be the opposite. This is where the grace of God comes in. I have heard testimonies of convicts who were transformed by the love of God and now live for Jesus every day. Their families, officers and other inmates testify of the change they have seen. Some of these people have committed grave offences, but some would say they took a life and deserve none. Before Jesus changed his life, Saul, who is now Apostle Paul, tortured and killed Christians, and he did it with zeal because he believed he was right. This is the same Apostle Paul that wrote most of the New Testament. God's forgiveness was more than enough to cleanse and restore him after all the terrible things he had done. This is a wonder of the love of God; it is the love He has for everyone. If you only knew the power and capability of God's love. Again, this is why we need it, because to forgive and to show compassion in such a situation would be impossible without knowing God's love first.

How to Love Each Other, God says:

1. Confess your trespasses to one another, and pray for

one another, that you may be healed. The effective, fervent prayer of a righteous man avails much. James 5:16

We should be able to go to each other in love and be received in love; reach out and be able to confide in and pray for one another.

2. By this all will know that you are my disciples if you have love one for another. John 13:35

The thing that identifies you as a disciple of Christ is the love you have for and show to one another. Jesus commanded His disciples to go into the world and make more disciples. How we treat each other is an example to the world of what a follower of Christ should be. If we are always tearing each other down, bickering and fighting amongst ourselves, the evidence is clear for all to see. You cannot teach something you don't know, so always be caught loving your neighbour because you don't know who is watching and learning from you.

3. *So we, being many, are one body in Christ, and individually members of one another. Romans 12:5*

We are united in Christ – united in faith and purpose. We are one body and just as a body has members (limbs, organs, bones - all with a specific purpose), so are we in the body of Christ, and we must be unified under one mind and one heart to function and succeed. A body whose members constantly fight against itself is good for nothing.

4. Be of the same mind toward one another. Do not set your mind on high things, but associate with the

humble. Do not be wise in your own opinion. Romans 12:16
Love is not proud or rude, nor does it think more highly of itself than it ought to. Treat all people well and do not discriminate. It is a natural reaction to treat people we think have 'high value' better than people we think are not. But God said, change your mind-set! All His people have value, and every soul is precious. The factors generally used to determine a person's value is usually education or circumstance, both of which are subject to change and should never dictate how we treat someone. The homeless person on the street should be treated with the same respect and compassion as anyone else.

5. Owe no one anything except to love one another, for he who loves another has fulfilled the law. Romans 13:8
According to the Dake reference bible, this scripture is not addressing 'just' debt such as mortgage or a bank loan (though you should pay your debts off as quickly as possible), it is saying that we have no obligation to people outside of civil authorities, but we are bound to them only by love, and the love God has commanded. Beware of obligation! There can be a sense of obligation between the brethren at times, particularly if you know the person well. You may feel you have to respond, give or help when they ask. Alternatively, you may make requests (reasonable or otherwise) from certain people because you know they won't say no. When we take advantage of each other it is a type of abuse, and it will cause division and strife. Love must be freely given and freely received.

If you are doing anything under any level of duress, know that you can say no, and be right. If you cannot say no without issue, you may have to rethink the depth of that connection. You 'must' do nothing; owe no one anything except Agape.

6. Bear one another's burdens, and so fulfil the law of Christ. Galatians 6:2
Support one another and build each other up. Do not be jealous of, or judge one another, but bear each other's burdens. Do not browbeat those who fall but remember we are all human and anyone can find themselves in a situation where they need compassion and grace.

7. *Be kind to one another, tender-hearted, forgiving one another, even as Christ forgave you. Ephesians 4:32*
Treat others well; be kind and supportive. Everyone is different but kindness will win-over every time. Sometimes people are in turmoil and at war with themselves and a kind word or gesture is like cool water on a hot day. In the book of Proverbs 15:1 God says,
A soft answer turns away wrath, but a harsh word stirs up anger (NKJV)

Use Wisdom
We must love others, but we shouldn't leave ourselves open and vulnerable. God says we are to be wise as serpents and protect ourselves, protect our minds and our hearts.

Keep your heart with all diligence, for out of it spring the issues of life. Proverbs 4:23

And the peace of God, which surpasses all understanding, will guard your hearts and your minds in Christ Jesus. Philippians 4:7

Jesus loved people and had compassion on them, but the bible says he did not 'give' himself to them. What does this mean. That we must have boundaries and we must be ready to defend ourselves when we need to. Self-defence does not cancel God's command to love, but God gives us wisdom in his Word, to know who, how and when to fight.

He teaches my hands to war... Psalm 18:34

We do not need to go on the offensive, God said, "vengeance is mine." However, we must be girded with spiritual and mental armour, ready to defend ourselves from the onslaught that may come. In the previous chapter, we learned about protecting ourselves and loving ourselves enough to create and maintain healthy boundaries. If those boundaries are challenged, you must, with wisdom, bring correction and remind them of those boundaries. As a last resort, also be prepared to part from their company. You can still have agape and part company and come to an agreement in your disagreement.

We are charged to protect the people and things God has given. In fact, God says, we are true believers when we do.

But if anyone does not provide for his own, and especially for those of his household, he has denied the faith and is worse than an unbeliever. 1 Timothy 5:8

Like a muddied fountain and a polluted spring, is a righteous man who yields and compromises his integrity before the wicked. Proverbs 25:26 (AMP)

In the book of Mathew, Jesus speaks of turning the other cheek, giving your cloak and going the extra mile. This type of surrender is in relation to loving your neighbour and sacrifice: giving up your rights (revenge or defence of self, comfort) for the good of someone else. You are justified to defend yourself and have the right to say no, but instead, demonstrate sacrifice and put the needs of others before your own. However, in Proverbs 25:26, we use it as a reference to compromise or sacrificing integrity. When we compromise who we are, our faith and the blessings we have received because of fear or pressure, God says, not only are we corrupted, but we are like a pollutant to the Body of Christ. God has given us His word to develop our faith and to stand and fight, if necessary, for what is right. If we then give up or "show our belly" as the saying goes, we 'fall down' before the wicked and we compromise the integrity of God's word, who He is and what He's done.

When a strong man, fully armed, guards his own palace, his goods are in peace. Luke 11:21

Loving others requires wisdom. Love others but do not leave yourself open to attack or abuse. Guard yourself;

put on the full armour of God.

Finally, be strong in the Lord and in his mighty power. Put on the full armour of God, so that you can take your stand against the devil's schemes...
Therefore, put on the full armour of God, so that when the day of evil comes, you may be able to stand your ground, and after you have done everything, to stand.
Ephesians 6:10-11, 13

In his book of the same name, Bishop Michael Hutton-Wood tells us Forgive but don't Forget. He encourages us to forgive others, but not to forget what they did; we must learn from it and use wisdom to ensure it doesn't happen again. There is another saying, fool me once shame on you, fool me twice shame on me. We have no control over the first time we are hurt by others, but if it happens again, it is because we did not learn from it and left ourselves vulnerable to repeat offences. God says there are 'fools' in this world and we must be wise, because they can cause problems in our lives. All the wisdom you need is found in His Word. God says, seek me, and use My wisdom and My word to fortify yourselves, so that you can go into the world and love others freely, also being fully equipped to stand during any difficulty.

JESUS IS LOVE

The embodiment of God's love is Jesus. Simultaneously, He *is* and *has* God's Spirit, Light and Love.

For God so loved the world that He gave His only begotten Son, that whoever believes in Him should not perish but have everlasting life. For God did not send His Son into the world to condemn the world, but that the world, through Him might be saved. John 3:16-17

In the beginning of this book, we talked about God's plan for us since the fall, and His desire to restore us to our rightful position and righteousness in Him. The culmination of our Father's efforts is the sacrifice of His Son, Jesus. For love of us, Jesus Christ was sent into the world to be an example in life, to save us through His death and to give us hope by His resurrection. Thus, proof of God's love was the sacrifice of His Son in our place. This is the nucleus of the Gospel and the one thing that the world sorely needs. The Love of God is life transforming, and God wants every person on earth to know His love, through His Son. If you have known this love, it is your responsibility to tell others.

What More Proof Do You Need?

People ask for proof of love all the time. When people question God's love for them, their lack of faith and understanding is an insult to the sacrifice. If you are ignorant, the slight may be less, but for those who have known the love of God, it is a greater insult.

And that servant, which knew his lord's will, and prepared not himself, neither did according to his will, shall be beaten with many stripes.

But he that knew not, and did commit things worthy of stripes, shall be beaten with few stripes. For unto whomsoever much is given, of him shall be much required: and to whom men have committed much, of him they will ask the more. Luke 12:47-48 (KJV)

God encourages us to 'remember' Him, who He is and everything he has done. We are not only to remember, but we are to teach our children and share it with others. In so doing, we not only build our faith, but we grow and mature in His love. We increase our capacity for love, which in turn increases our impact on those around us. Love is always present in every situation. The evidence is clear, but often we are too preoccupied with our feelings and circumstances to see.

God has done everything. There is nothing more to be done except for us to believe it, accept it and walk in it. Our society tends to have a more romanticised view of love. We see this in movies all the time, but sacrificial love is God's idea. If you think about it, the movies that stay with us and have the greatest impact, are the movies where the character is willing to sacrifice everything for their love, even their own lives.

...he poured out his life unto death and was numbered with the transgressors. For he bore the sin of many and made intercession for the transgressors. Isaiah 53:12 (NIV)

In Genesis 22, God tested not only Abraham's faith, He also tested Abraham's love. Was Abraham's love for his son greater than his love for God? Did he love and trust God so completely, that he would sacrifice His only son simply because God asked him to? God required proof.

Then God said, "Take now your son, your only son Isaac, whom you love, and go to the land of Moriah, and offer him there as a burnt offering on one of the mountains of which I shall tell you." So, Abraham rose early in the morning and saddled his donkey, and took two of his young men with him, and Isaac his son; and he split the wood for the burnt offering and arose and went to the place of which God had told him. Then on the third day Abraham lifted his eyes and saw the place afar off. And Abraham said to his young men, "Stay here with the donkey; the lad and I will go yonder and worship, and we will come back to you." So, Abraham took the wood of the burnt offering and laid it on Isaac his son; and he took the fire in his hand, and a knife, and the two of them went together. But Isaac spoke to Abraham his father and said, "My father!"

And he said, "Here I am, my son."

Then he said, "Look, the fire and the wood, but where is the lamb for a burnt offering?"

And Abraham said, "My son, God will provide for Himself the lamb for a burnt offering." So, the two of them went together. Then they came to the place of which God had told him. And Abraham built an altar there and placed the wood in order; and he bound Isaac his son and laid him on the altar, upon the wood. And Abraham stretched out his hand and took the knife to slay his son. But the Angel of the Lord called to him from heaven and said, "Abraham, Abraham!"

So, he said, "Here I am."

And He said, "Do not lay your hand on the lad, or do anything to him; for now, I know that you fear God, since you have not withheld your son, your only son, from Me." Genesis 22:2-12

There is a clear parallel between the sacrifice of Isaac and the sacrifice of Jesus. Abraham proved His love for God by sacrificing Isaac, as God proved His love for us by sacrificing His son Jesus. Abraham loved God more and gave up his son to prove it. God loves us more and gave up His Son to prove it. *Selah*.

The need for man's redemption was greater than God's private love for His Son Jesus. See how valuable you are! Do you understand how much God wants you? Saving you meant more to Him. Humanity has endured all this time because our Father refuses to let us go. You may have a hard time digesting this revelation. It is mind-blowing when you think on it, but this is yet another dimension, and a greater revelation of God's great love.

The Other Side

Let us look at this scripture from Isaac's point of view. Isaac was a young boy who was loved and favoured by his father. He would have been familiar with the customs and traditions of his family, because as the child destined to inherit, Abraham would have begun to train and groom him in the culture and the faith. That morning, though he wasn't told what they were doing and where they were going, once he saw the equipment they were carrying, he would have known immediately what it was for. Isaac asked Abraham, "Where is the sacrifice?" Strangely, Abraham did not tell him outright what God asked him to do and that Isaac was the intended sacrifice. Instead, he replied, "God will provide one." From what we know of Abraham, we can assume that even in this moment he hoped that God would change his mind, so he didn't bring finality to the situation by naming Isaac as the sacrifice. To sacrifice is a difficult thing to do and is an extreme test of the will. It is very painful, and given a choice, no one 'wants' to do it. To sacrifice takes faith, hope or love in, or love of something greater than yourself.

Esther risked her life to go before the king, because her duty and preservation of her people was greater than herself.

Daniel risked his life because as a captive in a foreign land, his freedom and the freedom of his people to freely worship God, was greater than himself.

Jesus went to the cross because the will of His Father was greater than himself. He gave his life because the will of Father God is greater than His own. In the Garden of Gethsemane he cried, *"let this cup [of suffering] pass from me, nevertheless, not my will, but thy will be done."*

Abraham did not want to sacrifice his son, as much as Isaac did not want to be the sacrifice. The scriptures say that Abraham bound him and placed him on the altar. This would mean Isaac surrendered and allowed his father to prepare him for sacrifice. Isaac could have run away from his father; Abraham was old, so he could have escaped, but he didn't. He stayed and trusted his father completely and laid down his life willingly. Jesus, like Isaac had complete trust in his Father, God. During His life, Jesus always spoke of His relationship with God the Father. Jesus said:

"Have I been with you so long, and yet you have not known Me, Philip? He who has seen Me has seen the Father; so how can you say, 'Show us the Father'? Do you not believe that I am in the Father, and the Father in Me? The words that I speak to you I do not speak on My own authority; but the Father who dwells in Me does the works. Believe Me that I am in the Father and the Father in Me, or else believe Me for the sake of the

works themselves. John 14:9-11

To obey the will of Father God was greater than His own will, and Jesus *chose* to lay down His life. This sacrifice, the death, burial and resurrection of Jesus, was the culmination of a plan that began at the fall in the book of Genesis; it is the climax of a love story that is still ongoing. The bible says in John 14:15:

"If you love Me, keep My commandments. And I will pray to the Father, and He will give you another Helper, that He may abide with you forever—the Spirit of truth, whom the world cannot receive, because it neither sees Him nor knows Him; but you know Him, for He dwells with you and will be in you. I will not leave you orphans; I will come to you.

Jesus asked God to send us a Helper that will be with us and live in us. We no longer need a priest or a temple to worship God, because we are connected to Him directly through the Holy Spirit. His love is alive in us, and we can tap into it daily, whenever we want, for whatever we need. God has given us everything we need to live an abundant and victorious life. He has done everything for us and there is nothing more to be done. Jesus said, **"It is finished!"**

There are no more sacrifices, no more substitutions, just our decision to accept what has been done. God has made it as simple as he can and now the ball is in our court. If you are ready, you can accept the gift of God's love right now; believe on the Son of God and invite Him into your heart.

Pray this:

Father, I repent of my sin, and I ask for your forgiveness. I am ready to receive all your love. Thank you for sending your Son Jesus to die for me. I believe in my heart, and I confess that Jesus Christ is the Son of God, and now Lord of my life. I receive your Holy Spirit to teach me and help me to live for you every day. Thank you for saving me. In Jesus name I pray, Amen.

What God Says About Love

IN CONCLUSION

This book scratches the surface of this subject; briefly breaking down the key concepts of Love, but hopefully it will be the springboard that launches you to a new level of awareness and ignites a desire in you to seek a deeper revelation of the fullness of God's Love. When we know the purpose of a thing, we will not abuse it. The better we know God, the better we can love Him ourselves and others.

My Prayer For You

I encourage you in your walk of faith, and I pray that God meets you wherever you are. May He flood your being with the light of His love, that you will be forever changed, and that having been filled, you will go out and pour into others. May God's glory be seen in your life, and may it touch everyone with whom you come in contact. May the light of His love continuously shine in the darkness through you, and may this world be better for having you in it.

God richly bless you.

THE LOVE SCRIPTURES

What God Says About Love

Therefore, know that the LORD your God, He is God, the faithful God who keeps covenant and mercy for a thousand generations with those who love Him and keep His commandments. Deuteronomy 7:9

You shall love the LORD your God with all your heart, with all your soul, and with all your strength. Deuteronomy 6:5

I will love You, O LORD, my strength. Psalms 18:1

Because he has set his love upon Me, therefore I will deliver him; I will set him on high, because he has known My name. Psalms 91:14

And I will delight myself in Your commandments, Which I love. My hands also I will lift up to Your commandments, Which I love, And I will meditate on Your statutes. Psalm 119:47

Hatred stirs up strife, but love covers all sins. Proverbs 10:12

What God Says About Love

He who spares his rod hates his son, but he who loves him disciplines him promptly. Proverbs 13:24

Since you were precious in My sight, you have been honoured, and I have loved you; Therefore, I will give men for you, And people for your life. Isaiah 43:4

The LORD has appeared of old to me, saying: "Yes, I have loved you with an everlasting love; Therefore, with loving kindness I have drawn you. Jeremiah 31:3

"When I passed by you again and looked upon you, indeed your time was the time of love; so, I spread My wing over you and covered your nakedness. Yes, I swore an oath to you and entered into a covenant with you, and you became Mine," says the Lord GOD. Ezekiel 16:8

You have heard that it was said, 'You shall love your neighbour and hate your enemy.' But I say to you, love your enemies, bless those who curse you, do good to those who hate you, and pray for those who spitefully use you and persecute you; for if you love those who love you, what reward have you? Do not even the tax collectors do the same. Matthew 5:43-46

What God Says About Love

Jesus said to him, 'You shall love the LORD your God with all your heart, with all your soul, and with all your mind.' And the second is like it: 'You shall love your neighbour as yourself.' Matthew 22:37-38

For God so loved the world that He gave His only begotten Son, that whoever believes in Him should not perish but have everlasting life. John 3:16-17

*A new commandment I give to you, that you love one another; as I have loved you, that you also love one another. By this all will know that you are My disciples, if you have love for one another."
John 13:34*

If you love Me, keep My commandments... He who has My commandments and keeps them, it is he who loves Me. And he who loves Me will be loved by My Father, and I will love him and manifest Myself to him. John 14:15, 21

As the Father loved Me, I also have loved you; abide in My love. If you keep My commandments, you will abide in My love, just as I have kept My Father's commandments and abide in His love. John 15:9-10

What God Says About Love

Greater love has no one than this, than to lay down one's life for his friends. John 15:13

Now hope does not disappoint, because the love of God has been poured out in our hearts by the Holy Spirit who was given to us.

...but God demonstrates His own love toward us, in that while we were still sinners, Christ died for us. Romans 5:5,8

Who shall separate us from the love of Christ? Shall tribulation, or distress, or persecution, or famine, or nakedness, or peril, or sword? As it is written: "For Your sake we are killed all day long. We are accounted as sheep for the slaughter. Yet in all these things we are more than conquerors through Him who loved us. For I am persuaded that neither death nor life, nor angels nor principalities nor powers, nor things present nor things to come, nor height nor depth, nor any other created thing, shall be able to separate us from the love of God which is in Christ Jesus our Lord." Romans 8:35-39

What God Says About Love

Be kindly affectionate to one another with brotherly love, in honour giving preference to one another...
Romans 12:10

Beloved, do not avenge yourselves, but rather give place to wrath; for it is written, "Vengeance is Mine, I will repay," says the Lord. Romans 12:19

Owe no one anything except to love one another, for he who loves another has fulfilled the law. For the commandments, "You shall not commit adultery," "You shall not murder," "You shall not steal," "You shall not bear false witness," "You shall not covet," and if there is any other commandment, are all summed up in this saying, namely, "You shall love your neighbour as yourself." Love does no harm to a neighbour; therefore, love is the fulfilment of the law.
Romans 13:8-10

Though I speak with the tongues of men and of angels, but have not love, I have become sounding brass or a clanging cymbal. And though I have the gift of prophecy, and understand all mysteries and all knowledge, and though I have all faith, so that I could remove mountains, but have not love, I am nothing.
1 Corinthians 13:1-2

What God Says About Love

Let all that you do be done with love.
1 Corinthians 16:14

So let each one give as he purposes in his heart, not grudgingly or of necessity; for God loves a cheerful giver. 2 Corinthians 9:7

I have been crucified with Christ; it is no longer I who live, but Christ lives in me; and the life which I now live in the flesh I live by faith in the Son of God, who loved me and gave Himself for me. Galatians 2:20

For you, brethren, have been called to liberty; only do not use liberty as an opportunity for the flesh, but through love serve one another. For all the law is fulfilled in one word, even in this: "You shall love your neighbour as yourself." Galatians 5:13-14

I beseech you to walk worthy of the calling with which you were called, with all lowliness and gentleness, with longsuffering, bearing with one another in love, endeavouring to keep the unity of the Spirit in the bond of peace. Ephesians 4:2

What God Says About Love

And walk in love, as Christ also has loved us and given Himself for us, an offering and a sacrifice to God for a sweet-smelling aroma. Ephesians 5:1

Nevertheless, let each one of you so love his own wife as himself, and let the wife see that she respects her husband. Ephesians 5:33

And this I pray, that your love may abound still more and more in knowledge and all discernment... Philippians 1:9

But above all these things put on love, which is the bond of perfection. Colossians 3:14

And may the Lord make you increase and abound in love to one another and to all, just as we do to you, so that He may establish your hearts blameless in holiness before our God and Father at the coming of our Lord Jesus Christ with all His saints. 1 Thessalonians 3:12-13

What God Says About Love

Be at peace among yourselves. 1 Thessalonians 5:13

*Now may the Lord direct your hearts into the love of God and into the patience of Christ.
2 Thessalonians 3:5*

Now the purpose of the commandment is love from a pure heart, from a good conscience, and from sincere faith... 1 Timothy 1:5

For God has not given us a spirit of fear, but of power and of love and of a sound mind. 2 Timothy 1-7

We ourselves were also once foolish, disobedient, deceived, serving various lusts and pleasures, living in malice and envy, hateful and hating one another. But when the kindness and the love of God our Saviour toward man appeared, not by works of righteousness which we have done, but according to His mercy He saved us, through the washing of regeneration and renewing of the Holy Spirit... Titus 3:3-5

What God Says About Love

You have loved righteousness and hated lawlessness; Therefore God, Your God, has anointed you with the oil of gladness more than Your companions." Hebrews 1:9

For God is not unjust to forget your work and labour of love which you have shown toward His name, in that you have ministered to the saints, and do minister. Hebrews 6:10

For whom the LORD loves He chastens and scourges every son whom He receives." Hebrews 12:6

Blessed is the man who endures temptation; for when he has been approved, he will receive the crown of life which the Lord has promised to those who love Him. James 1:12

Listen, my beloved brethren: Has God not chosen the poor of this world to be rich in faith and heirs of the kingdom which He promised to those who love Him? James 2:5

What God Says About Love

If you really fulfil the royal law according to the Scripture, "You shall love your neighbour as yourself," you do well. James 2:8

Since you have purified your souls in obeying the truth through the Spirit in sincere love of the brethren, love one another fervently with a pure heart...1 Peter 1:22

Finally, all of you be of one mind, having compassion for one another; love as brothers, be tender-hearted, be courteous. 1 Peter 3:8

And above all things have fervent love for one another, for "love will cover a multitude of sins." 1 Peter 4:8

Greet one another with a kiss of love. Peace to you all who are in Christ Jesus. Amen. 1 Peter 5:14

But whoever keeps His word, truly the love of God is perfected in him. By this we know that we are in Him. 1 John 2:5

He who loves his brother abides in the light, and there is no cause for stumbling in him. 1 John 2:10

Do not love the world or the things in the world. If anyone loves the world, the love of the Father is not in him. 1 John 2:15

Behold what manner of love the Father has bestowed on us, that we should be called children of God! Therefore, the world does not know us, because it did not know Him. 1 John 3:1

By this we know love, because He laid down His life for us. And we also ought to lay down our lives for the brethren. But whoever has this world's goods, and sees his brother in need, and shuts up his heart from him, how does the love of God abide in him? 1 John 3:16

My little children, let us not love in word or in tongue, but in deed and in truth. 1 John 3:18

What God Says About Love

Beloved, let us love one another, for love is of God; and everyone who loves is born of God and knows God. He who does not love does not know God, for God is love. 1 John 4:7-8

Beloved, if God so loved us, we also ought to love one another. 1 John 4:11

No one has seen God at any time. If we love one another, God abides in us, and His love has been perfected in us. 1 John 4:12

And we have known and believed the love that God has for us. God is love, and he who abides in love abides in God, and God in him. Love has been perfected among us in this: that we may have boldness in the day of judgment; because as He is, so are we in this world. 1 John 4:16

There is no fear in love; but perfect love casts out fear, because fear involves torment. He who fears has not been made perfect in love. 1 John 4:18

We love Him because He first loved us. 1 John 4:19

If someone says, "I love God," and hates his brother, he is a liar; for he who does not love his brother whom he has seen, how can he love God whom he has not seen? 1 John 4:20

Whoever believes that Jesus is the Christ is born of God, and everyone who loves Him who begot also loves him who is begotten of Him. 1 John 5:1

By this we know that we love the children of God, when we love God and keep His commandments. For this is the love of God, that we keep His commandments. And His commandments are not burdensome. 1 John 5:2-3

Mercy, peace, and love be multiplied to you. Jude 1:2

Keep yourselves in the love of God, looking for the mercy of our Lord Jesus Christ unto eternal life. Jude 1:21

What God Says About Love

...and from Jesus Christ, the faithful witness, the firstborn from the dead, and the ruler over the kings of the earth. To Him who loved us and washed us from our sins in His own blood...Revelation 1:5

As many as I love, I rebuke and chasten. Therefore, be zealous and repent. Revelation 3:19

Yes, I have loved you with an everlasting love...

www.ingramcontent.com/pod-product-compliance
Lightning Source LLC
Chambersburg PA
CBHW070938180426
43192CB00039B/2324